THIS IS
AUSTRALIA

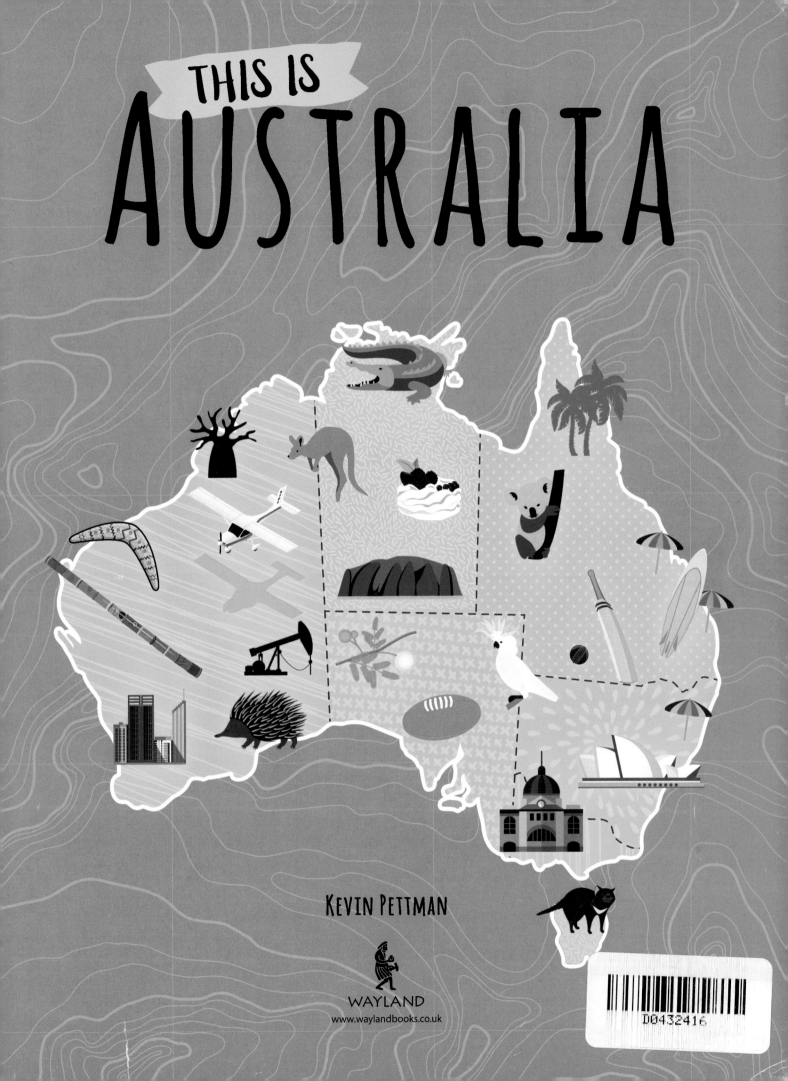

Kevin Pettman

WAYLAND
www.waylandbooks.co.uk

First published in 2018 by Wayland
Copyright © Hodder and Stoughton, 2018

Written by Kevin Pettman
Design by Simon Letchford
Edited by Catherine Brereton

ISBN: 978 1 5263 0454 4

Wayland, an imprint of
Hachette Children's Group
Part of Hodder and Stoughton
Carmelite House
50 Victoria Embankment
London EC4Y 0DZ

An Hachette UK Company
www.hachette.co.uk
www.hachettechildrens.co.uk

Printed in China
10 9 8 7 6 5 4 3 2 1

Picture acknowledgements (cover and inside pages): All images and graphic elements used are courtesy of Shutterstock. Every attempt has been made to clear copyright. Should there be any inadvertent omission, please apply to the Publisher for rectification.

The website addresses (URLs) listed in this book were valid at the time of going to press. However, it is possible that the contents or addresses may have changed since the publication of this book. No responsibility for any such changes can be accepted by either the author or the Publisher.

Contents

Welcome to Australia

Australia is one of the most interesting, ancient and exciting places in the world. It's the sixth largest country, in size, and is also an island and a continent. Australia is full of fun facts and fascinating people …

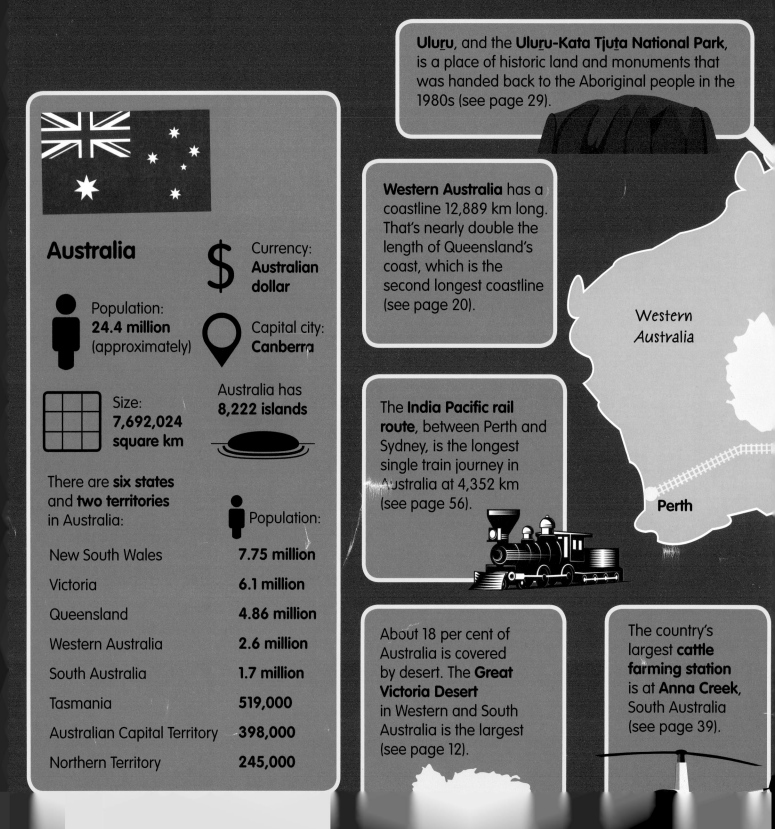

Uluru, and the **Uluru-Kata Tjuta National Park**, is a place of historic land and monuments that was handed back to the Aboriginal people in the 1980s (see page 29).

Western Australia has a coastline 12,889 km long. That's nearly double the length of Queensland's coast, which is the second longest coastline (see page 20).

The **India Pacific rail route**, between Perth and Sydney, is the longest single train journey in Australia at 4,352 km (see page 56).

About 18 per cent of Australia is covered by desert. The **Great Victoria Desert** in Western and South Australia is the largest (see page 12).

The country's largest **cattle farming station** is at **Anna Creek**, South Australia (see page 39).

Western Australia

Perth

Australia

Currency: **Australian dollar**

Population: **24.4 million** (approximately)

Capital city: **Canberra**

Size: **7,692,024 square km**

Australia has **8,222 islands**

There are **six states** and **two territories** in Australia:

	Population:
New South Wales	**7.75 million**
Victoria	**6.1 million**
Queensland	**4.86 million**
Western Australia	**2.6 million**
South Australia	**1.7 million**
Tasmania	**519,000**
Australian Capital Territory	**398,000**
Northern Territory	**245,000**

Aboriginal rock art, east of Darwin in Arnhem Land, is around 18,000 years old (see page 22).

The **Great Barrier Reef**, off the coast of Queensland, is the largest reef system in the world. It covers over 2,000 islands, nearly 3,000 separate reefs and thousands of plant and fish species (see page 48).

Rainforests on the east coast have trees that are over 2,500 years old (see page 58).

Darwin

Northern Territory

The Wheel of Brisbane attraction is nearly 60 m tall and opened in 2008 (see page 34).

Queensland

Uluru-Kata Tjuta National Park

Sydney, in New South Wales, is the **largest city** in Australia with approximately 5 million people. Over **8 million visitors** explore the famous Sydney Opera House each year (see page 8).

Brisbane

Great Victoria Desert

South Australia

Anna Creek

New South Wales

Sydney

ACT

Canberra

Victoria

Melbourne

Koalas live in eastern and southern coastal areas of Australia. Their favourite (and only!) food is eucalyptus leaves (see page 15).

Parliament House, Canberra, is the home of the Australian government (see page 26).

Tasmania

Hobart

Theatre Royal in Hobart, Tasmania, opened in 1837 and is Australia's oldest working theatre (see page 22).

The **Melbourne Cricket Ground** is the biggest sports stadium in Australia. It can hold 100,000 people (see page 24).

Great dates

The Australian rocks and landscape began to form about 4.5 billion years ago. Australia's human history is bursting with many stories and events. Take a look at these key dates in the country's history.

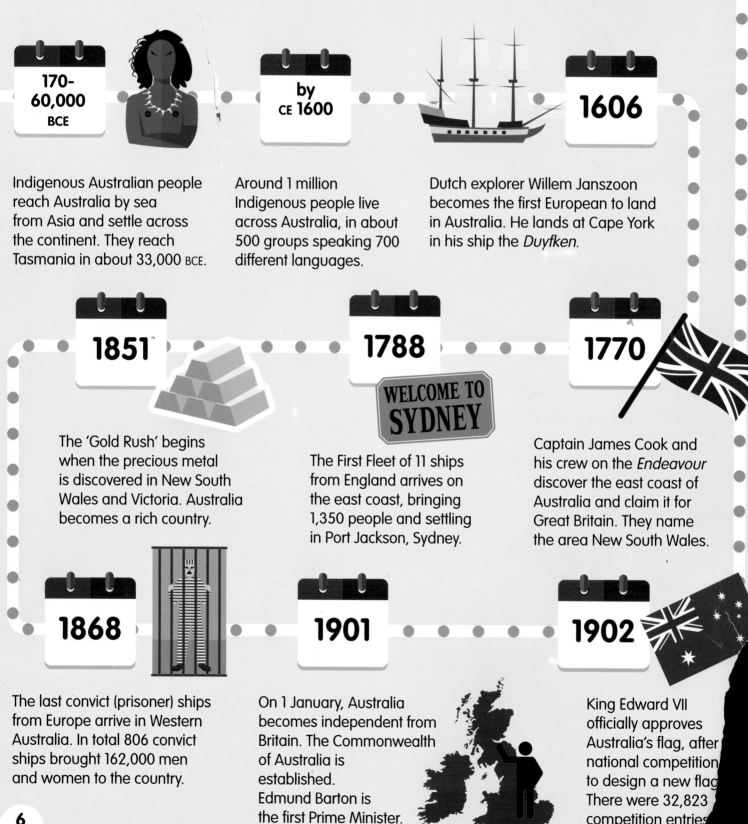

170-60,000 BCE

Indigenous Australian people reach Australia by sea from Asia and settle across the continent. They reach Tasmania in about 33,000 BCE.

by CE 1600

Around 1 million Indigenous people live across Australia, in about 500 groups speaking 700 different languages.

1606

Dutch explorer Willem Janszoon becomes the first European to land in Australia. He lands at Cape York in his ship the *Duyfken*.

1851

The 'Gold Rush' begins when the precious metal is discovered in New South Wales and Victoria. Australia becomes a rich country.

1788

WELCOME TO SYDNEY

The First Fleet of 11 ships from England arrives on the east coast, bringing 1,350 people and settling in Port Jackson, Sydney.

1770

Captain James Cook and his crew on the *Endeavour* discover the east coast of Australia and claim it for Great Britain. They name the area New South Wales.

1868

The last convict (prisoner) ships from Europe arrive in Western Australia. In total 806 convict ships brought 162,000 men and women to the country.

1901

On 1 January, Australia becomes independent from Britain. The Commonwealth of Australia is established. Edmund Barton is the first Prime Minister.

1902

King Edward VII officially approves Australia's flag, after a national competition to design a new flag. There were 32,823 competition entries.

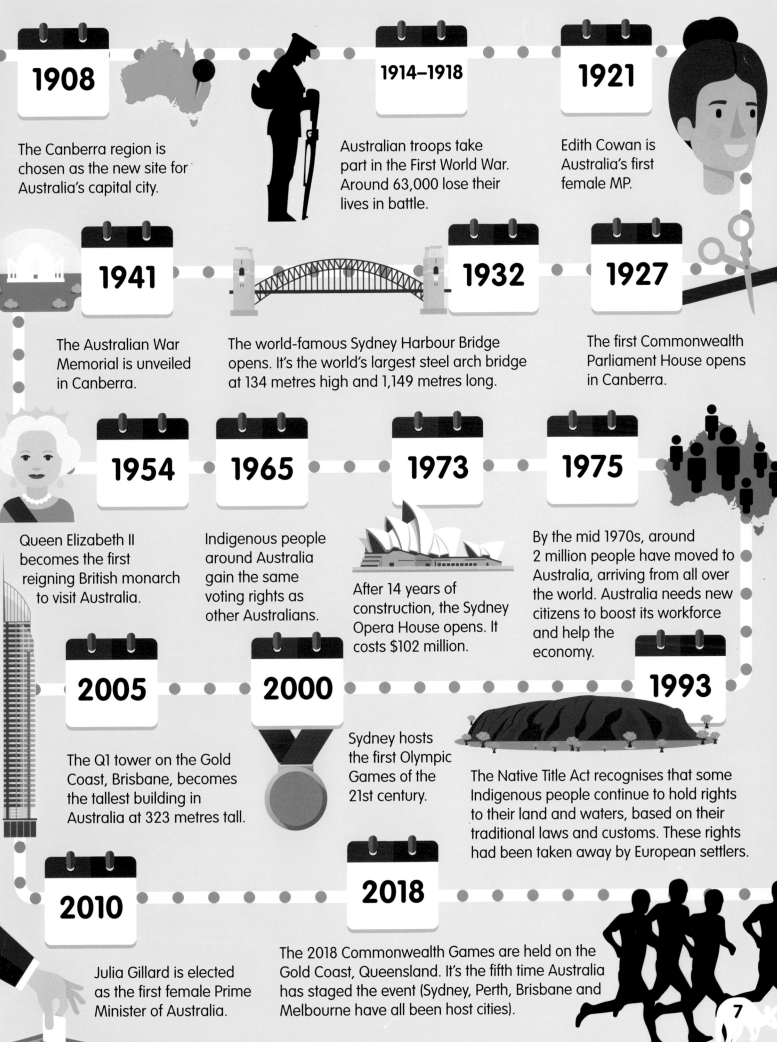

1908

The Canberra region is chosen as the new site for Australia's capital city.

1914–1918

Australian troops take part in the First World War. Around 63,000 lose their lives in battle.

1921

Edith Cowan is Australia's first female MP.

1941

The Australian War Memorial is unveiled in Canberra.

1932

The world-famous Sydney Harbour Bridge opens. It's the world's largest steel arch bridge at 134 metres high and 1,149 metres long.

1927

The first Commonwealth Parliament House opens in Canberra.

1954

Queen Elizabeth II becomes the first reigning British monarch to visit Australia.

1965

Indigenous people around Australia gain the same voting rights as other Australians.

1973

After 14 years of construction, the Sydney Opera House opens. It costs $102 million.

1975

By the mid 1970s, around 2 million people have moved to Australia, arriving from all over the world. Australia needs new citizens to boost its workforce and help the economy.

2005

The Q1 tower on the Gold Coast, Brisbane, becomes the tallest building in Australia at 323 metres tall.

2000

Sydney hosts the first Olympic Games of the 21st century.

1993

The Native Title Act recognises that some Indigenous people continue to hold rights to their land and waters, based on their traditional laws and customs. These rights had been taken away by European settlers.

2010

Julia Gillard is elected as the first female Prime Minister of Australia.

2018

The 2018 Commonwealth Games are held on the Gold Coast, Queensland. It's the fifth time Australia has staged the event (Sydney, Perth, Brisbane and Melbourne have all been host cities).

Icons of Australia

From famous sights such as Sydney Harbour Bridge to famous landscapes such as the wild outback, from boomerangs and didgeridoos to surfers and flying doctors, there are lots of things people think of when they think of Australia.

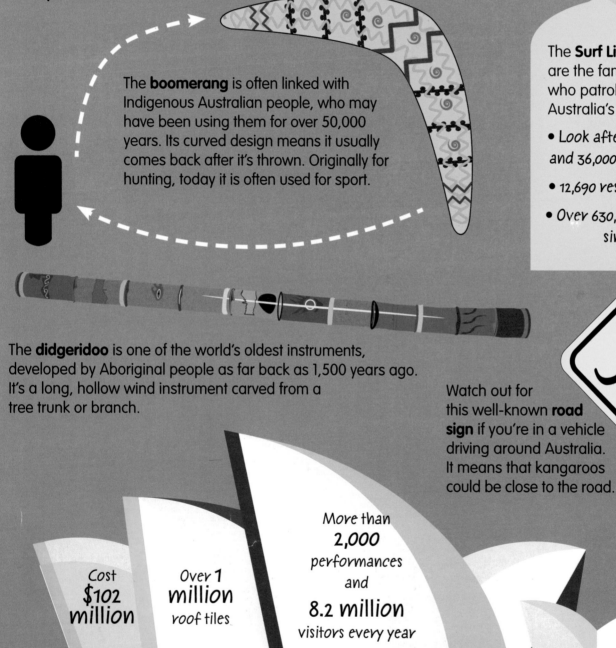

The **boomerang** is often linked with Indigenous Australian people, who may have been using them for over 50,000 years. Its curved design means it usually comes back after it's thrown. Originally for hunting, today it is often used for sport.

The **Surf Life Saving** group are the famous volunteers who patrol many of Australia's beaches.

- Look after 12,000 beaches and 36,000 km of coastline
- 12,690 rescues every year
- Over 630,000 people saved since 1907

The **didgeridoo** is one of the world's oldest instruments, developed by Aboriginal people as far back as 1,500 years ago. It's a long, hollow wind instrument carved from a tree trunk or branch.

Watch out for this well-known **road sign** if you're in a vehicle driving around Australia. It means that kangaroos could be close to the road.

Cost **$102 million**

Over **1 million** roof tiles

More than **2,000** performances and **8.2 million** visitors every year

The iconic **Sydney Opera House**, on Sydney Harbour, took 14 years to build. It was opened by Queen Elizabeth in 1973.

In 2016, its 68 aircraft covered **26,157,502 km**, which is the same as **34** trips to the Moon and back!

Set up in 1928, the **Royal Flying Doctor Service** helps patients in remote areas all over Australia.

The outback is Australia's wild landscape, far from towns and cities. Australians and visitors alike love exploring its wide open spaces.

The **cork hat** is thought to have been worn by some Australian workers in the outback in the 19th and 20th centuries.

Corks dangling from the hat move around and help keep flies and other insects away.

50 km

The **Cape Byron Lighthouse**, in New South Wales, was built in 1901 and is the most easterly lighthouse in Australia. It's also the country's most powerful, with a range of 50 km.

A **yowie** is a wild ape-like creature that legends say lives in remote places around Australia. But is it real?

There's a statue of a yowie in the town of Kilcoy, Queensland.

Around **70 million** sheep are shorn every year in Australia. The nation is the world's largest wool producer, creating 284,000 tonnes a year.

Sydney Harbour Bridge opened in 1932. It's the world's largest steel arch bridge at 134 metres high and 1,149 metres long.

Approximately **180,000** vehicles use the bridge every day.

City living

Australia is full of vast open spaces, but it's also home to some of the most exciting and beautiful cities in the world. Check out these fascinating facts all about city living around Australia.

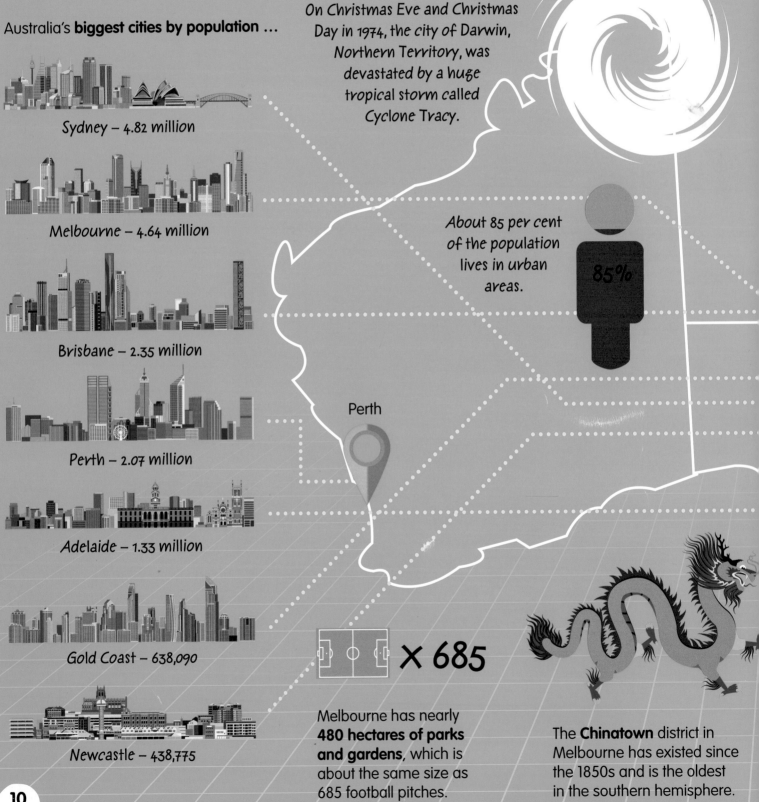

Australia's **biggest cities by population** …

Sydney – 4.82 million

Melbourne – 4.64 million

Brisbane – 2.35 million

Perth – 2.07 million

Adelaide – 1.33 million

Gold Coast – 638,090

Newcastle – 438,775

Darwin

On Christmas Eve and Christmas Day in 1974, the city of Darwin, Northern Territory, was devastated by a huge tropical storm called Cyclone Tracy.

About 85 per cent of the population lives in urban areas.

85%

Perth

× 685

Melbourne has nearly **480 hectares of parks and gardens**, which is about the same size as 685 football pitches.

The **Chinatown** district in Melbourne has existed since the 1850s and is the oldest in the southern hemisphere.

33.3 years – Darwin and the surrounding Greater Darwin area has the **youngest** average age population in Australia's capital cities.

Australia's first **post office** was opened by Isaac Nichols at his home on George Street, Sydney, in 1809.

A house on New South Head Road, by Sydney Harbour, became Australia's most expensive home in 2017 when it sold for about **$75 million.**

Nearly 70 per cent of Australia's population lives in the state or territory capital cities of Canberra, Sydney, Melbourne, Brisbane, Darwin, Adelaide, Perth and Hobart.

70%

Streets Beach, on the South Bank area in Brisbane, is Australia's only inner city, man-made beach. It has white sandy shores, a lagoon and tropical plants.

Brisbane

Gold Coast

Newcastle

Gold Coast, a major city to the south of Brisbane, is the host of the **Commonwealth Games** sports event in April 2018.

Adelaide

Sydney

Canberra

Melbourne

In 1911, American architects Walter and Marion Griffin were given the task of designing the modern city of **Canberra**.

Hobart

39.8 years – Hobart and the surrounding Greater Hobart area has the **oldest** average age population.

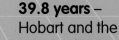

In the 1830s, the area where Melbourne is now was called 'Batmania', after the Australian explorer John Batman.

Canberra was chosen as **Australia's national capital** in 1908. It has over 300,000 residents and is the country's largest inland city.

Amazing landscapes and environments

Australia is known for its flat and dry environments. But its vast lands also take in rainforests, wetlands, mountains, extinct volcanoes, ancient rocks and even a few ski resorts!

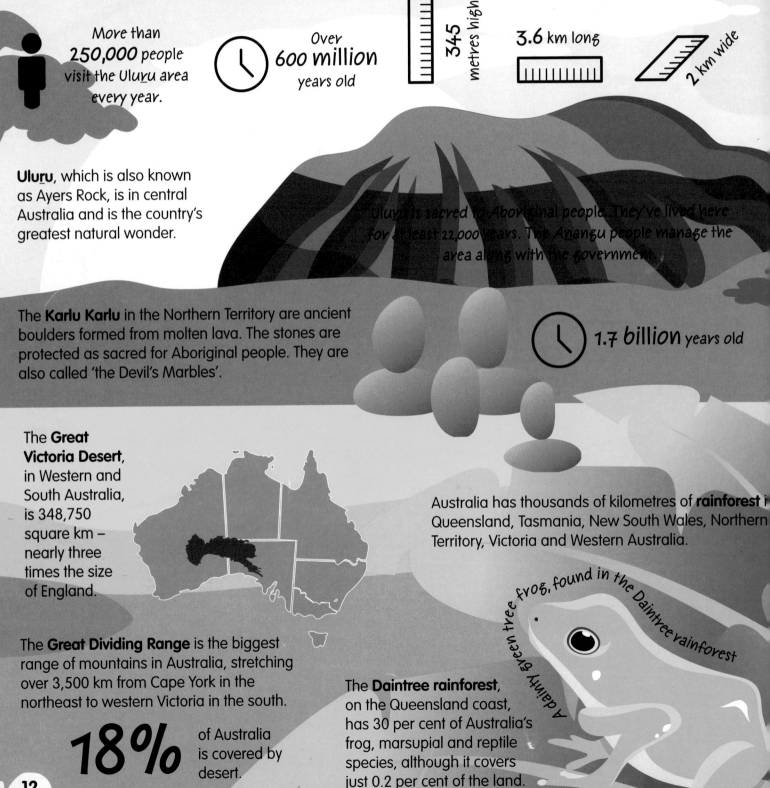

More than **250,000 people** visit the Uluru area every year.

Over **600 million** years old

345 metres high

3.6 km long

2 km wide

Uluru, which is also known as Ayers Rock, is in central Australia and is the country's greatest natural wonder.

Uluru is sacred to Aboriginal people. They've lived here for at least 22,000 years. The Anangu people manage the area along with the government.

The **Karlu Karlu** in the Northern Territory are ancient boulders formed from molten lava. The stones are protected as sacred for Aboriginal people. They are also called 'the Devil's Marbles'.

1.7 billion years old

The **Great Victoria Desert**, in Western and South Australia, is 348,750 square km – nearly three times the size of England.

Australia has thousands of kilometres of **rainforest** in Queensland, Tasmania, New South Wales, Northern Territory, Victoria and Western Australia.

The **Great Dividing Range** is the biggest range of mountains in Australia, stretching over 3,500 km from Cape York in the northeast to western Victoria in the south.

18% of Australia is covered by desert.

A dainty green tree frog, found in the Daintree rainforest

The **Daintree rainforest**, on the Queensland coast, has 30 per cent of Australia's frog, marsupial and reptile species, although it covers just 0.2 per cent of the land.

Australia's diverse landscape even lets you go **skiing** between June and October.

Top 5 ski resorts:

Perisher, New South Wales

Falls Creek, Victoria

Thredbo, New South Wales

Mount Buller, Victoria

Mount Hotham, Victoria

Mount Warning, on the coast of New South Wales, is an extinct **volcano** that last erupted 20 million years ago. It's the first place on the Australian mainland to catch the morning sun.

Tharwa

The famous **Australian Alps Walking Track** stretches for 650 kilometres from Walhalla, Victoria, to Tharwa, near Canberra.

Crosses three states, four national parks and Australia's highest peaks

Takes 50–60 days to walk

Walhalla

151 kilometres (94 miles)

That's the actual length of Ninety Mile Beach, in the far southeast of Australia. It's the third-longest beach in the world.

268 metres

The height of Wallaman Falls, in northern Queensland. It's the highest single-drop waterfall in the country.

390 metres

The depth of Niggly Cave in Tasmania. It's thought to be the deepest in Australia and is part of the Junee Florentine Valley Caves Complex.

Lake Mungo, in southeast Australia, is a vast dry lake that was full of water for 40,000 years. In the 1960s, the skeletal remains of an Aboriginal person were found and nicknamed **Mungo Man**. The remains could be 50,000 years old.

I've got a bone to pick with you!

13

Awesome animals

Australia is home to some of the planet's most amazing, beautiful, rare and dangerous animals. From koalas to kangaroos, dingoes to dolphins and snakes to spiders, it's a land packed with curious creatures.

There are 55 **kangaroo and wallaby** species native to Australia. Estimates suggest there are between 50 and 60 million in the country – more than double Australia's human population.

The average eastern grey kangaroo is 1.3 m tall and lives for eight to 10 years.

60 kg

Of the 334 **marsupial** species in the world, Australia is home to over 200. A marsupial is a mammal that usually carries newborn babies in its pouch. Australia's marsupials include kangaroos, wombats, Tasmanian devils, koalas and possums.

The **platypus** lives in lakes, streams and rivers in eastern Australia and Tasmania. This bizarre creature, a mammal that lays eggs, can grow up to 60 cm and weigh 2 kg.

When a platypus skin was sent to London in 1798, the British Museum thought it was a joke, believing no animal could look like this.

In north Queensland's rainforests, two species of kangaroo live in trees. These are the Lumholtz tree kangaroo and the Bennett's tree kangaroo.

Some 'tree-roos' jump from heights of 20 metres to the ground.

Australia has 21 of the world's top 25 most poisonous snakes. These include ... inland taipan ... eastern brown snake ... coastal taipan ... eastern states tiger snake ... red-bellied black snake.

Migrating birds such as sandpipers, stints, plovers and curlews make huge trips from the northern hemisphere to feed in Australia.

The country has over 170 species of **snake**. The scrub python is the longest, growing to 5 metres.

- Weighs up to 1 kg
- Can fly 50 km per night
- Wingspan of nearly 1 m

Australia has around 80 types of **bat**. One type is known as the 'flying fox'.

There are an estimated **24 million pets** in Australian households, including:

4.2 million **birds**

3.6 million **dogs**

2.7 million **cats**

8.7 million **fish**

4.8 million **other**

Two types of **crocodile** live in northern Australia

Freshwater crocodile: only found in Australia and usually less than 3 metres long.

3 m

6 m

Estuarine (salt water) crocodile: the largest reptile in the world, with the biggest males measuring 6 metres.

Monkey Mia Beach, in Western Australia, is a famous spot where visitors like to feed wild bottlenose **dolphins** in the shallow waters.

The **dingo** is Australia's wild dog. It arrived in Australia about 4,000 years ago. It's common in most of the mainland.

The dingo howls but doesn't bark.

The **emu** originates from Australia. It's the largest bird in the country and can grow to 1.9 metres tall.

48 kph

Koalas live in eastern Australia and southern coastal areas. They are very laid-back animals.

Wombats are strong, stocky and can grow to around 1 metre long. They are some of the best burrowers in the world, creating underground tunnels up to 30 metres long and 5 metres deep.

Koalas sleep or rest for about 20 hours a day.

They eat eucalyptus leaves, which take 200 hours to digest.

They have a small brain that doesn't fill their skull.

26,000 kilometres is the distance some birds fly to reach Australia.

15

Famous faces

From sportspeople to singers, actors to artists, Australia's most famous faces are recognised all over the world. Here are just a few Aussie stars.

Cathy Freeman (born 1973) was the first Indigenous Australian athlete to win a gold medal at the Commonwealth Games, which she did in 1990 aged just 16. At the 2000 Olympics in Sydney, she won gold in the 400 metres and celebrated by waving both the Aboriginal and the Australian flags.

After shooting to fame around the world in the 1980s by starring in popular TV show *Neighbours*, **Kylie Minogue** (born 1968) soon became an international pop icon. From Melbourne, Kylie has sold over 80 million records worldwide and has had many number one songs (10 in Australia).

Animal lover **Steve Irwin** (1962–2006) was a TV star, watched by millions on his show Crocodile Hunter. Steve inspired people to respect and protect wildlife, especially dangerous animals like crocodiles and snakes. He was sadly killed by a stingray while filming.

Queenie McKenzie (1915–1998) was one of the most famous Indigenous Australian artists. She spent her entire life living, working and painting in the Kimberley, Western Australia, and finally displayed her artistic skills in the late 1980s and 1990s. She was an important figurehead for Indigenous people.

Famous fact!
Actor Chris Hemsworth (born 1983) was born in Melbourne and is famous as the superhero Thor.

Famous fact!
Actor Hugh Jackman (born 1968) is best known for playing the superhero Wolverine in the *X-Men* films.

Famous fact!
Nicole Kidman (born 1967) is an Oscar-winning actor and one of Australia's most famous movie stars.

Famous fact!
Cate Blanchett (born 1969) was Galadriel in *Lord of the Rings* and is the only Australian actor to have won two Oscars.

Famous fact!
Rebel Wilson (born 1980) is an actor and writer known for her hilarious comedy performances.

Legendary cricketer **Sir Donald Bradman** (1908–2001) is Australia's greatest sportsman. He played cricket for 21 years and captained the Australia and South Australia Sheffield Shield team. Over 94,000 fans watched his last game in December 1948 at the Melbourne Cricket Ground.

In total Don Bradman made an amazing 28,067 first-class runs.

Famous fact!

Bradman is the only Australian cricketer to be knighted and made a 'Sir'.

Fantastic food and drink

From Vegemite to delicious meat pies and ANZAC biscuits, Australia produces and consumes a fascinating mixture of food and drink. Here are some tasty facts, stats and stories that will have you licking your lips!

moo!

The word '**barbecue**' became popular in Australia in the 1920s. It referred to roasting an animal outdoors at a public event.

Famous spread **Vegemite** was developed in 1922 by Australian food technologist Dr Cyril P Callister.

- Over 22 million jars are sold every year

- In 1928 its name was changed to Parwill, but it changed back in the 1930s

The meringue and fruit dessert **pavlova** is thought to have been created by Herbert Sachse at Hotel Esplanade, Perth, in the late 1920s. The dish was named in honour of the visiting Russian ballet dancer **Anna Pavlova**.

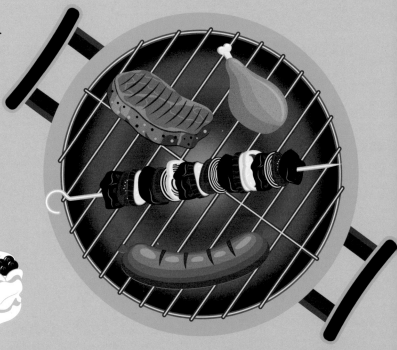

The famous **Four'N Twenty meat pies** were first made in 1947. The company now makes more than **50,000** pies an hour.

In 1934 the Royal Australian Air Force at Laverton, Melbourne, held an air display and roasted **27 cattle** to feed the **200,000** people who attended.

Home-baked biscuits sold to raise funds for First World War soldiers became known as **ANZACs**. ANZAC means Australian and New Zealand Army Corps.

The biscuits, made of rolled oats, sugar, flour, butter, golden syrup and bicarbonate of soda, were popular because they lasted well and didn't contain eggs, which were rationed. Most recipes now contain coconut too.

ANZAC biscuit are traditionally made on ANZAC day – 25 April.

There are about 60 **wine-producing** regions around the country. The biggest vineyards are in South Australia, Victoria and New South Wales.

- Over 100 countries sell wines from Australia

- The UK imports more wine from Australia than from France

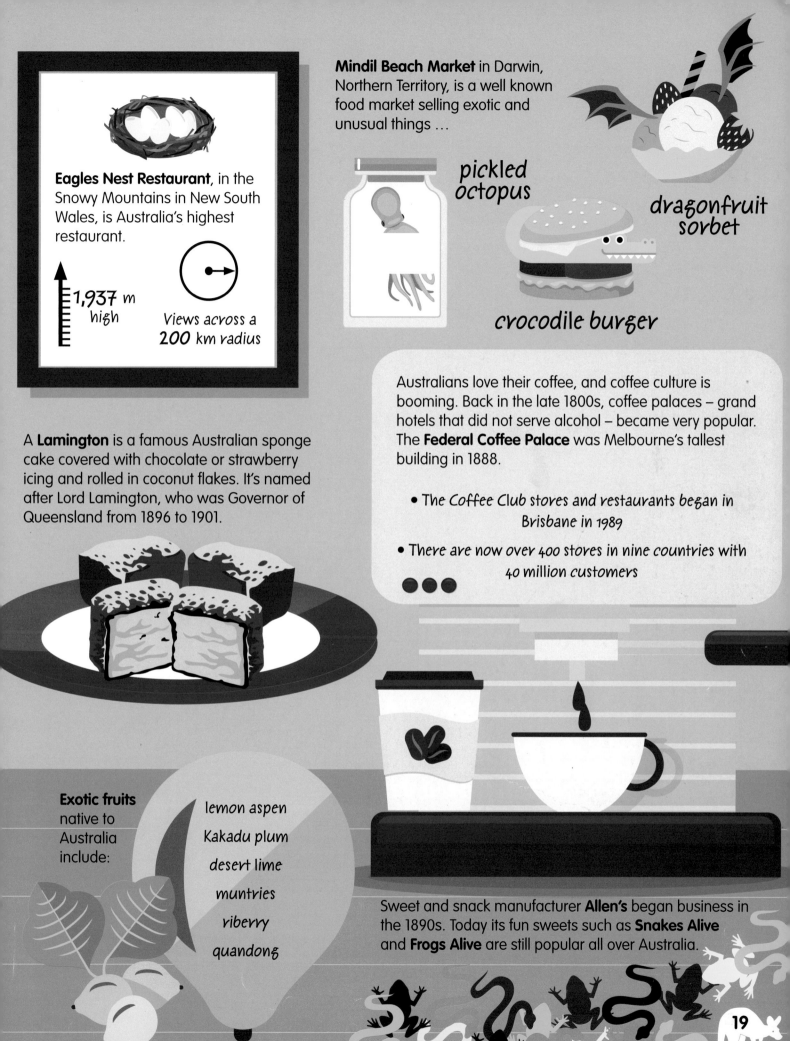

Eagles Nest Restaurant, in the Snowy Mountains in New South Wales, is Australia's highest restaurant.

1,937 m high

Views across a **200 km radius**

Mindil Beach Market in Darwin, Northern Territory, is a well known food market selling exotic and unusual things …

pickled octopus

dragonfruit sorbet

crocodile burger

A **Lamington** is a famous Australian sponge cake covered with chocolate or strawberry icing and rolled in coconut flakes. It's named after Lord Lamington, who was Governor of Queensland from 1896 to 1901.

Australians love their coffee, and coffee culture is booming. Back in the late 1800s, coffee palaces – grand hotels that did not serve alcohol – became very popular. The **Federal Coffee Palace** was Melbourne's tallest building in 1888.

- The Coffee Club stores and restaurants began in Brisbane in 1989

- There are now over 400 stores in nine countries with 40 million customers

Exotic fruits native to Australia include:

lemon aspen

Kakadu plum

desert lime

muntries

riberry

quandong

Sweet and snack manufacturer **Allen's** began business in the 1890s. Today its fun sweets such as **Snakes Alive** and **Frogs Alive** are still popular all over Australia.

19

Coast to coast

Australia's coastline seems to be never-ending, and it's full of wonderful beaches and attractions. It's packed with interest, from surfing and sharks to shipwrecks and cockle shells.

Australia's coastline is an incredible **36,735 kilometres** long. It has over **7,000** beaches, which is more than any other country. Australia's islands have more than **23,000 kilometres** of coastline.

Coastline length

Western Australia	**12,889 km**
Queensland	**6,973 km**
Northern Territory	**5,437 km**
South Australia	**3,816 km**
Tasmania	**2,833 km**
New South Wales	**2,007 km**
Victoria	**1,868 km**
Australian Capital Territory	**0 km**

Australia is the world's sixth-largest country and the only one in the top six that is also an island.

6th

10 m high

Cable Beach, in Western Australia, is popular with visitors who enjoy **camel rides** along the sand and watching the sun set over the Indian Ocean.

Shell Beach, in the Shark Bay Marine Park, is 60 kilometres long and made up of tiny cockle shells in layers up to 10 metres high.

Whale of a time

A coastal bay called Head of Bight, in South Australia, is a great spot to watch **southern right whales** between May and October.

38 DAYS, 21 HOURS, 41 MINUTES, 42 SECONDS
The world record Bruce Arms set in 2011 for sailing solo around Australia.

Gordons Bay, Sydney, has a 500-m underwater nature trail for divers.

Whitehaven Beach, on Whitsunday Island in Queensland, is often called the prettiest beach in Australia.

• 7 km long
• The bright white sand is 98 per cent silica, which has very fine grains

75 Mile Beach is a beach on Fraser Island, Queensland, that's 75 miles (120 km) long.

It's not a safe place to swim because of dangerous currents and sharks.

The Australian National Maritime Museum in Sydney has a replica of Captain Cook's **Endeavour** ship, which reached Australia in 1770.

33 M long **39 M** high and weighs **397** tonnes

Sunshine Coast, Queensland
• 60 km of coastline
• 3.2 million visitors a year

The are more than **100 beaches** around the urban area of **Sydney.**

$300 million

The value of the bluefin tuna fishing industry around Port Lincoln, South Australia. This area is said to be Australia's seafood fishing capital.

Gold Coast, Queensland
• 70 km of coastline
• 10 million visitors a year

BEACH

The largest **shipwreck** in Australian waters was that of *HMAS Australia*, which was deliberately sunk 50 kilometres from Sydney in 1924.

I'll try and play in tuna

Port Lincoln has a big festival each year, with musicians and performers, called Tunarama.

180 m long 19,000 tonnes

A land of culture

Australia has a small population compared to the UK, the USA and many Asian countries, but it's a land bursting with exciting and fascinating culture. From ancient arts to modern theatre, poetry and singing there's something to interest everyone.

The Concert Hall is the largest venue inside the **Sydney Opera House**, with 2,679 seats.

More than **4,000** Aboriginal rock engravings are recorded around Australia. In the Sydney–Hawkesbury area there's a whale engraving **20 metres long**.

Aboriginal rock art in the Arnhem Land, a vast territory east of Darwin, dates back 18,000 years.

Theatre Royal in Hobart, Tasmania, is Australia's oldest working theatre and opened in 1837.

A fire destroyed the stage in 1984 and cost $1 million to repair.

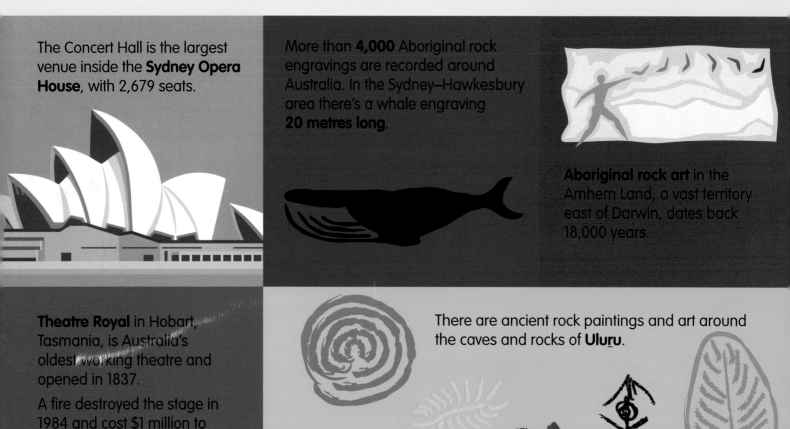

There are ancient rock paintings and art around the caves and rocks of **Uluṟu**.

Perth International Arts Festival began in 1953.

3,000

The estimated number of paintings Indigenous Australian artist **Emily Kame Kngwarreye** (1910–1996) painted in just eight years. That's about one every day.

Advance Australia Fair officially became the country's **national anthem** in 1984, replacing God Save the Queen.

It was first sung in Sydney in 1878 by a choir of 10,000 people.

A B 'Banjo' Paterson (1864–1941) is one of Australia's most popular poets. He wrote about everyday life in rural areas.

'Waltzing Matilda', 'The Man from Snowy River' and 'Clancy of the Overflow' are his three most famous poems.

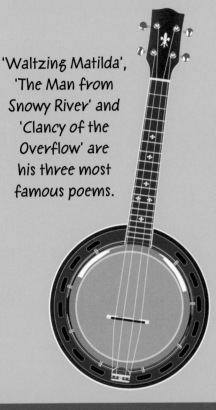

Henry Handel Richardson

The name that popular female Australian writer, **Ethel Richardson**, published her books under in the 20th century.

Chinese culture has influenced Australia since the 1850s, when Chinese people came to Victoria during the gold rush. A change to immigration policies in the 1970s also saw more people settle from China.

In 1973, English-born Australian writer **Patrick White** was the first Aussie to win the Nobel Prize for Literature. The Nobel Prize is one of the top awards for a writer.

The Museum of Chinese Australian History, in Melbourne, has five floors displaying the cultural links between the two countries.

Queen's Theatre, Adelaide, is the oldest purpose-built theatre on the Australian mainland.

- Opened in 1840
- Shakespeare's Othello was the theatre's first production

Greeks have a long cultural history with Australia. Thousands migrated in the 19th century and again after the Second World War (1939–1945).

The design of Melbourne's Shrine of Remembrance was influenced by the Mausoleum of Halicarnassus, in Greece, one of the Seven Wonders of the World.

Some famous Australian singers:
- Kylie Minogue
- Dannii Minogue
- Sia
- Delta Goodrem
- Gurrumul Yunupingu
- John Farnham
- Michael Hutchence

Gurrumul Yunupingu was a blind musician who played several instruments and sang about his Aboriginal background and connection with the land. He passed away in 2017, aged 46.

200 million

The number of music albums rock band **AC/DC** have sold. The band was formed by Australian musicians Malcolm and Angus Young in 1973.

Australian playwright **David Williamson** has written about 50 theatre plays, 18 films and nine TV shows or series.

Super sport

Australia is a nation that loves sport, whether that's competing or supporting their heroes. Cricket, rugby, Australian rules football, tennis, athletics, swimming, soccer and lots more are very popular in this sport-obsessed country.

The Australian Football League (AFL) began in 1897 with eight founding teams:

Collingwood	Melbourne
Essendon	South Melbourne
Fitzroy	Carlton
Geelong	St Kilda

Australia was the first country to win the **Rugby World Cup** twice. They won it in 1991 and 1999.

George Gregan played a record 139 rugby union games for Australia between 1994 and 2007.

The Ashes is a famous cricket contest between Australia and England, played every three to four years. It began in 1882 and, up to the 2015 contest, both countries had won it 32 times.

×8

Australia won eight gold medals at the 2016 Olympics. The women's team won the first ever rugby sevens event.

In 1861 at Flemington Racecourse in Melbourne, the first **Melbourne Cup** horse race was held. It's one of the richest horse races in the world, with the owner of the winning horse receiving about **$3.6 million**.

$3.6 million

Melbourne Cricket Ground

- Largest sports stadium in Australia with 100,000 capacity
- Built in 1853 and staged first cricket game in 1854
- Set in Melbourne's Yarra Park, close to the city centre

Ian Thorpe is Australia's most successful swimmer. At the 2000 and 2004 Olympics he won a total of five gold medals, three silver and a bronze.

Thorpe is nicknamed 'Thorpedo' because of his speed through the water.

Tennis stars Roy Emerson and Rod Laver won 23 Grand Slam singles titles between them in the 1960s. Emerson won 12 and Laver 11.

American Serena Williams served

263 kph

on her way to win the 2017 Australian Open finals.

Legendary Australian golf player **Greg Norman** was nicknamed The Great White Shark because of his aggressive style on the course.

Norman won The Open Championship in 1986 and 1993.

The **Australian Open** is one of the world's four big 'Grand Slam' tennis events.

- **$3.7 million** prize to the singles winners in 2017
- **40,000** tennis balls are used in the tournament each year
- A record **728,763** fans watched the tournament in Melbourne Park in 2017

Talented athlete **Ellyse Perry** played for the women's national soccer and cricket teams when she was just 16 years old.

The Australian national soccer team is nicknamed the **Socceroos**.

In 2006, Tim Cahill scored the Socceroos' first ever goal at a FIFA World Cup finals.

The **Tour Down Under** is Australia's number one road bike race. Australian rider **Richie Porte** won it for the first time in 2017.

The **Australian Grand Prix**, in Melbourne, is traditionally the first F1 race of the season.

Sir Jack Brabham became the first Australian to win the F1 world championship in 1959. He won it again in 1960 and 1966.

Brilliant buildings

Australia has hundreds of interesting and world-famous buildings throughout its vast land. These brilliant buildings were built from way back in 1799 to just a few years ago.

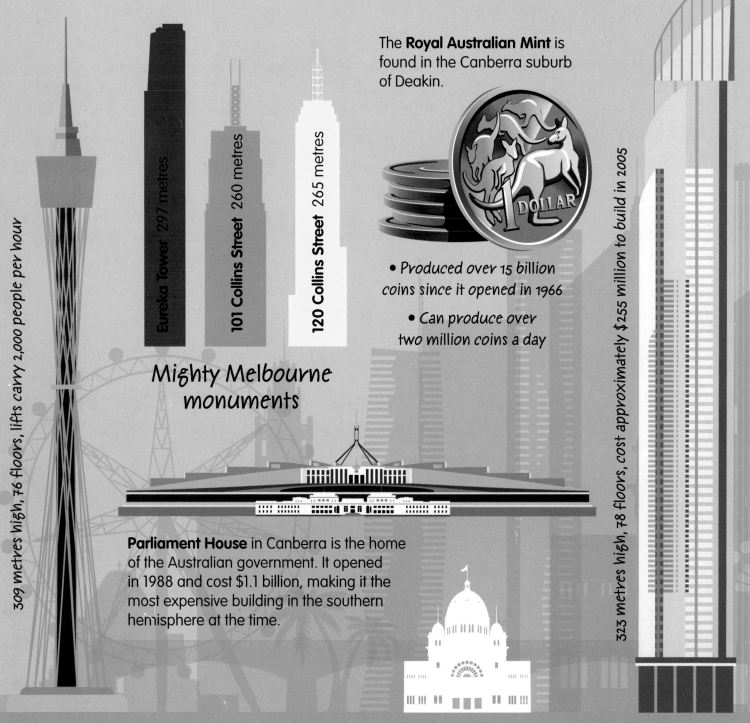

The **Royal Australian Mint** is found in the Canberra suburb of Deakin.

- Produced over 15 billion coins since it opened in 1966
- Can produce over two million coins a day

Eureka Tower 297 metres

101 Collins Street 260 metres

120 Collins Street 265 metres

Mighty Melbourne monuments

309 metres high, 76 floors, lifts carry 2,000 people per hour

323 metres high, 78 floors, cost approximately $255 million to build in 2005

Parliament House in Canberra is the home of the Australian government. It opened in 1988 and cost $1.1 billion, making it the most expensive building in the southern hemisphere at the time.

The **Sydney Tower** observation tower was completed in 1981.

The **Royal Exhibition Building** in Melbourne was opened in 1880. In 2004 it was the first Australian building to get UNESCO World Heritage status.

The **Q1** residential tower in Gold Coast, Brisbane, is the tallest building in Australia.

The **Alice Springs Telegraph Station** is a set of basic buildings in Alice Springs, deep in the centre of Australia, established in 1871.

It linked up communication cables to carry Alice Springs' first communication with England.

1799

Old Government House in Parramatta, New South Wales, is Australia's oldest surviving public building.

Government House is the oldest surviving building in Darwin, dating back to 1871. The building has survived …

bombing raids

The 82-metre high **Bell Tower** building in Perth has the oldest bell in Australia, called the Upton Grey Bell. It was made in 1550 in England and shipped to Australia in 2010.

cyclones

earthquakes

infestations of white ants

Inside the huge **Powerhouse Museum** in Sydney, which originally opened as a power station in 1902, visitors to the Zero Gravity Space Lab can experience weightlessness like an astronaut.

Over 10,000 construction workers helped to create the Sydney Opera House between 1959 and 1973.

…uilding 8, at the Royal Melbourne Institute of Technology, has a colourful and …riking design. Its outer walls have lots of different shapes, patterns and lines.

Indigenous Australian people

The Aboriginal and Torres Strait Islander people have lived in Australia for thousands of years. They treat the land as very special and have lots of customs, cultures and traditions. But unfortunately Indigenous Australian people have not always lived an easy life in Australia.

Indigenous Australians are believed to have lived all over Australia for at least **60,000 years**, possibly as far back as **170,000 years** ago.

In the 21st century an estimated **3 per cent** of the country's population are Aboriginal and Torres Strait Islander people.

Europeans settled in Australia in the 18th century. They often fought with the Aboriginal people, treating them badly and taking their land.

In the 18th century there were an estimated 750,000 Aboriginal people, speaking at least 300 languages.

There are about **500 different Aboriginal nations** in Australia, each with their own territory and language. The **Pitjantjatjara** people, who live close to Uluru, are the biggest language group.

CERTIFICATE

this certificate is proudly presented to

Signature   signature

Body painting can show things such as a community's location or a person's position in their group, or tells a story. It can vary from colourful patterns to white ash.

The **Native Title Act 1993** is a law that gave Aboriginal people rights to lands which were taken away from them by Europeans in the 1800s and 1900s.

1971

Neville Bonner became Australia's first Aboriginal MP. Since then 38 Indigenous Australian people have served in Parliament.

28

The **Australian Aboriginal Flag** was designed by Harold Thomas, a Luritja man of Central Australia, in 1971.

Black represents the Aboriginal people

Yellow represents the sun

Red represents the earth

- Developed the boomerang as a hunting tool
- Could follow and track animal footprints in the desert
- Remembered how to get back home after hunting

Ceremony is a traditional festival of Aboriginal spirits.

- Usually held at night
- Involves singing and dancing
- People dress with face paints, animal skins and feather
- An instrument called a didgeridoo (also known as a yidaki) is played.

Aboriginal people believe the land was created during **The Dreaming**, when their ancestors came from under the earth and walked around. When they walked they sang, and this singing created the land we now call Australia.

1985

Uluṟu, and the Uluṟu-Kata Tjuṯa National Park, was handed back to the Aboriginal people by the government. It's now jointly managed by the local Anangu people and the government.

1987

Writer **Sally Morgan** released her bestselling book, *My Place*, all about her family's struggles as Indigenous Australian people in this country.

2008

Prime Minister **Kevin Rudd** made a speech apologising for past mistreatment of Indigenous Australian peoples, especially the Stolen Generations, who were taken away from their families and raised by white families or in care homes.

Weather watch

Australia is a land of extremes. In the tropical zone in the north the temperature can reach 50°C in the wet season, and in the southeast it can drop to below freezing on high ground. From tropical downpours to cyclones and snowstorms, Australia's weather is amazingly varied.

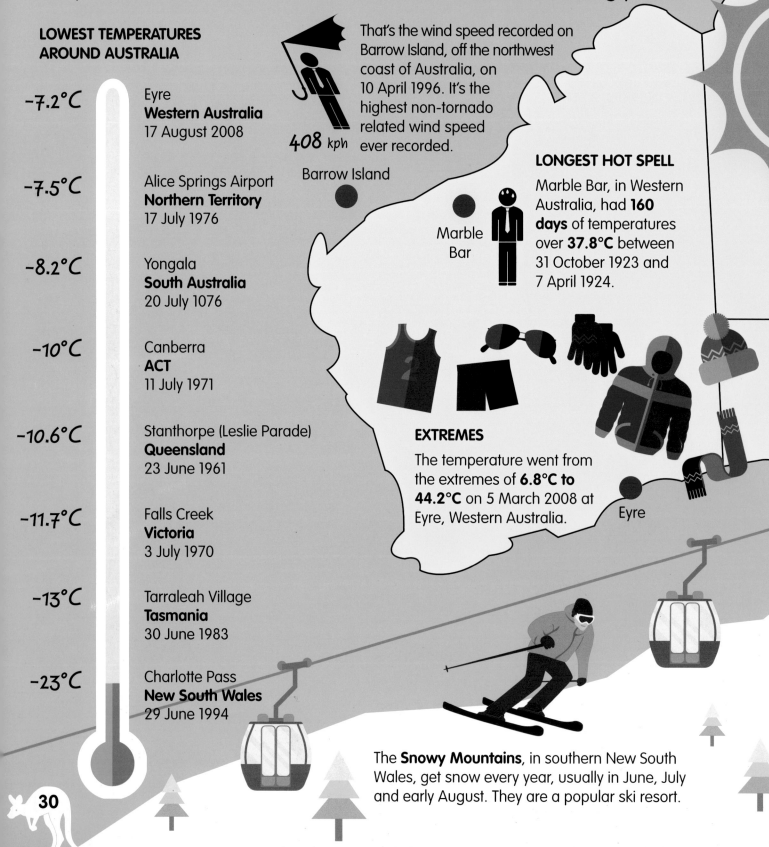

LOWEST TEMPERATURES AROUND AUSTRALIA

−7.2°C
Eyre
Western Australia
17 August 2008

−7.5°C
Alice Springs Airport
Northern Territory
17 July 1976

−8.2°C
Yongala
South Australia
20 July 1076

−10°C
Canberra
ACT
11 July 1971

−10.6°C
Stanthorpe (Leslie Parade)
Queensland
23 June 1961

−11.7°C
Falls Creek
Victoria
3 July 1970

−13°C
Tarraleah Village
Tasmania
30 June 1983

−23°C
Charlotte Pass
New South Wales
29 June 1994

That's the wind speed recorded on Barrow Island, off the northwest coast of Australia, on 10 April 1996. It's the highest non-tornado related wind speed ever recorded.

408 kph

Barrow Island

Marble Bar

LONGEST HOT SPELL

Marble Bar, in Western Australia, had **160 days** of temperatures over **37.8°C** between 31 October 1923 and 7 April 1924.

EXTREMES

The temperature went from the extremes of **6.8°C** to **44.2°C** on 5 March 2008 at Eyre, Western Australia.

Eyre

The **Snowy Mountains**, in southern New South Wales, get snow every year, usually in June, July and early August. They are a popular ski resort.

The **Bureau of Meteorology** is Australia's national weather, climate and water agency. It has eight State and Territory offices and 16 field stations that record and monitor things like rainfall, temperature, wind speed and humidity.

WETTEST PLACE

Bellenden Ker, in north Queensland, receives an average of **7,950 mm** of rain each year.

Bellenden Ker

DRIEST PLACE

Lake Eyre, in South Australia, gets just **125 mm** of rain per year on average.

Lake Eyre

The **highest daily rainfall** recorded in Australia was in Crohamhurst, on the coast of Queensland. A cyclone struck on 3 February 1893 and 907 mm of rain fell.

Crohamhurst

Snowy Mountains

On 7 February 2009, a huge bushfire began in Victoria during a heat wave.

- 173 people killed and 414 injured
- Winds of 100 kph spread the flames
- 3,500 buildings burned
- The day was called Black Saturday

Australia has an average rainfall each year of just **165 mm.**

HIGHEST TEMPERATURES AROUND AUSTRALIA

Oodnadatta Airport
South Australia
2 January 1960 — **50.7°C**

Mardie
Western Australia
19 February 1998 — **50.5°C**

Menindee Post Office
New South Wales
10 January 1939 — **49.7°C**

Birdsville Police Station
Queensland
24 December 1972 — **49.5°C**

Hopetoun Airport
Victoria
7 February 2009 — **48.8°C**

Finke Post Office
Northern Territory
1 January 1960 — **48.3°C**

Scamander
Tasmania
30 January 2009 — **42.2°C**

Canberra
ACT
1 February 1968 — **42.2°C**

Weird, wonderful and wacky

It's time to check out some unbelievable, outrageous and 'out of this world' facts and stories all about the bizarre side to Australia.

5,614 km

The length of the Dingo Fence in Queensland and South Australia. It's designed to keep dingoes away from farmland and is the **longest fence in the world**.

Deep Space Station 46 is a 26-metre-wide satellite, which was based at Honeysuckle Creek Tracking Station near Canberra. It beamed the first TV pictures to Earth of Neil Armstrong walking on the Moon in 1969.

Aaargh! I've been shot in the Sydney!

In 1868, **Prince Alfred** was the first British royal to visit Australia. He was shot in an attempted assassination in Sydney, but recovered.

Queen Elizabeth II visited Australia 16 times between 1954 and 2011.

The word '**selfie**', meaning a picture of yourself taken with a camera or phone, was thought to be first posted online by an Australian called Nathan Hope in 2002.

750,000

That's the estimated number of wild camels that roam the outback regions of Western Australia, South Australia, Queensland and Northern Territory.

Mamungkukumpurangkuntjunya Hill

in South Australia is officially the longest place name in the country.

The **Sydney Harbour Bridge** needs **30,000 litres** of paint to cover it. That's enough to cover about 60 soccer pitches.

Parap (Darwin), Tumut (New South Wales) and Glenelg (Adelaide) are all **palindromes**, which means their name reads the same forwards and backwards.

10

AS

An image of Englishman **Francis Greenway** used to appear on the **$10 note**. That's strange because in 1814 he was sent to Australia as a prisoner for illegally reproducing financial documents!

10 million
That's how many items the National Library of Australia buildings in Canberra holds.

Lake Hillier, on Middle Island off the south coast of Western Australia, is **pink**. It's thought the colour comes from bacteria living in the salt crusts.

Missed!

In the **Emu War** of 1932, the Royal Australian Artillery were sent to bring down emu populations, because the emus were eating farmers' crops and damaging fences. The emus won!

The Museum and Art Gallery of the Northern Territory (Darwin) has a 5-metre-long stuffed **crocodile**. The animal, called Sweetheart, was caught in 1979 in the Finniss River.

Monuments and sculptures

These structures, statues, sculptures and monuments are some of the most special – and strange – in Australia. From giant wheels and water fountains to tiny cats and prehistoric dinosaur footprints, Aussies adore them all!

The **Wheel of Brisbane** monument and attraction opened in 2008 and has 42 capsules that rise to almost 60 metres.

- *Ride lasts 12 minutes and rotates four times*
- *Eight people can fit in each capsule*

More than **3,300 dinosaur footprints** are on display at the Dinosaur Stampede National Monument in Queensland.

Formed **95 million** *years ago*

Cover an area of **210 sq m**

 A statue of **Trim the cat** sits at the foot of the Matthew Flinders statue in Sydney. Flinders, with his cat, sailed around Australia in the early 1800s.

 A little bronze statue of a terrier dog called **Islay** is outside the Queen Victoria Building in Sydney. Islay was a favourite pet of Queen Victoria.

There's a Captain James Cook memorial **water fountain** in Canberra. The fountain shoots water 114 metres high.

The **Queen Victoria** statue was originally on display in Dublin, Ireland, before being shipped to Sydney in the 1980s.

The first statue of **Captain James Cook**, the English sailor who landed in Australia in 1770, was erected in Sydney in 1874.

7 m tall

34

Oi, that tickles!

The Shrine of Remembrance in Melbourne honours the 89,000 Victorians who fought overseas, and the 19,000 who died, in the First World War.

Repainted in 2017 with paint brushes on 3 m poles

Larry the Lobster is a huge statue of a lobster next to a seafood restaurant in Kingston, South Australia. It's 17 metres high, which is nearly the height of two houses.

The Big Merino is a giant sheep statue in Goulburn, New South Wales, made from steel and concrete.

- 18 m long and 15.2 m high
- Weighs 100 tonnes
- Took six months to build

William Ricketts Sanctuary

Over **90** artistic **sculptures of Aboriginal people** are carved into tree trunks and rocks in the William Ricketts Sanctuary in Mount Dandenong, Victoria.

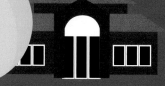

Tamworth, New South Wales, is the capital of Australia's country music scene. The Big Golden Guitar Tourist Centre has a **12-metre-high** fibreglass and steel **guitar model**, which weighs half a tonne.

The Big Pineapple in Queensland is one of several Australian 'Big Things'. Visitors can climb the pineapple, explore the nearby rainforest and find out all about pineapple farming.

16 m

Battling nation

Australian soldiers have taken part in many major wars and conflicts in the 20th and 21st centuries. The Air Force, Navy and ground troops serve in Australia and all over the world.

25 April 1915

ANZAC (Australian and New Zealand Army Corps) troops landed in **Gallipoli,** Turkey, to help Britain, France and Russia battle the Ottoman Empire during the First World War.

The **Victoria Cross for Australia** is Australia's highest honour and is awarded for acts of wartime bravery. It was created in 1991 and just four soldiers have been awarded it.

Gallipoli battle lasted for 8 months

8,141 killed or died of wounds

18,000 injured

Australia in the First World War (1914–1918)

331,000 soldiers fought

63,000 soldiers died

152,000 soldiers wounded

Australia in the Second World War (1939–1945)

1,000,000 soldiers fought

37,500 soldiers died

60,000 soldiers wounded

The **Australian War Memorial** was opened in 1941 in Canberra. It displays the names of **102,600** Australians killed in action. The Tomb of the Unknown Soldier honours an unknown soldier recovered from France, and represents all those who died and have no known grave.

The **Royal Australian Air Force** (RAAF) was set up in 1921.

The F/A-18F Super Hornet jet fighter can reach **1,960 kph**

Every day around the world between 500–700 RAAF people are involved in military and peacekeeping operations.

1942

In this year during the Second World War, Japanese planes bombed Darwin and its ships fired at Sydney and Newcastle.

Japanese submarines sunk Australian ship *HMAS Kuttabul* in Sydney Harbour.

A black labrador dog called Sarbi was awarded lots of medals for serving with the Australian Special Forces Explosive Detection Unit.

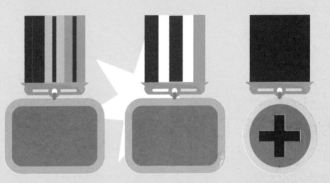

War Dog Operational Medal

Canine Service Medal

RSPCA Purple Cross Award

During the First World War, the British government bought all of Australia's exports of **wool**, **meat**, **wheat**, **butter** and **cheese** to help the UK fight against Germany and its allies.

In the 1960s and 1970s Australia fought in the **Vietnam War**, in southeast Asia. It was the first time Australia fought in a war without Britain.

500

Australian soldiers died

49

The number of ships, boats and submarines in the Royal Australian Navy in 2016.

Fantastic farming

Australia is one of the world's most important farming countries. It produces a wide variety of crops, from wheat and barley to sugar and sunflowers, as well as huge amounts of wool, beef and wine.

About **two thirds of Australia's land** is used for **farming** production.

- 90 per cent is used for grazing, which is land that livestock and animals feed on

- 314,000 sq km is used for growing crops – an area bigger than Italy

$50^{bn}

The value of Australia's farm production.

Australian farmers supply
93 per cent
of Australia's food.

Percentage of Australian workforce employed in **agriculture**:
1901 = 14%
2016 = 2.6%

A few months after the British settled in **1788**, Australia's livestock count was only:

7 cattle

7 horses

74 pigs

209 fowls

35 ducks

5 rabbits

18 turkeys

29 geese

29 sheep

There are about **140 million sheep** in Australia. That's **six times** more than the human population!

On average it takes a sheep shearer two minutes to take the wool off.

Australia's wool industry is worth over $2 billion a year.

Australia **exports** much of the food it produces, which means it sells it to other countries.

67 per cent of wheat exported

70 per cent of sugar exported

57 per cent of barley exported

Australia produces **1.9 million** bales of **cotton** each year.

Grows enough cotton to clothe 500 million people

Fibres from one 227 kg bale can make 4,300 pairs of socks

18 m

Giant combine harvesters with headers **18 metres long** operate on Australian wheat fields. The 'header' is the wide part of the combine that cuts the crops.

Elizabeth Farm, in the Sydney suburb of Parramatta, has Australia's **oldest surviving home**. The farm's original bungalow was built in **1793**.

Better take the helicopter!

The **Australian Agricultural Company** was established in 1824 and is the oldest Australian company that's still trading today.

Over 500,000 beef cattle at its farms and plants

The company's beef feeds over 1 million people every day

Sells $489 million worth of beef each year

23,000 sq km

The largest **cattle station** in Australia is at Anna Creek in South Australia. It's bigger than the country of Wales!

Southern Queensland, around the town of Allora, is famous for its many **sunflower fields**. Tourists take selfies next to sunflowers that can be **1.5 metres tall**.

Fish, oysters and kangaroo meat were the main foods in the Sydney area in the early 1800s.

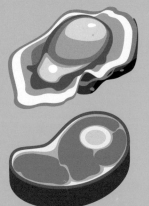

Incredible islands

Mainland Australia is a huge island nearly 4,000 kilometres wide, but Australia also includes thousands of small islands. Many are part of Australia itself and many are external territories – some are so far away they're actually in Asia, or are closer to Antarctica than Australia!

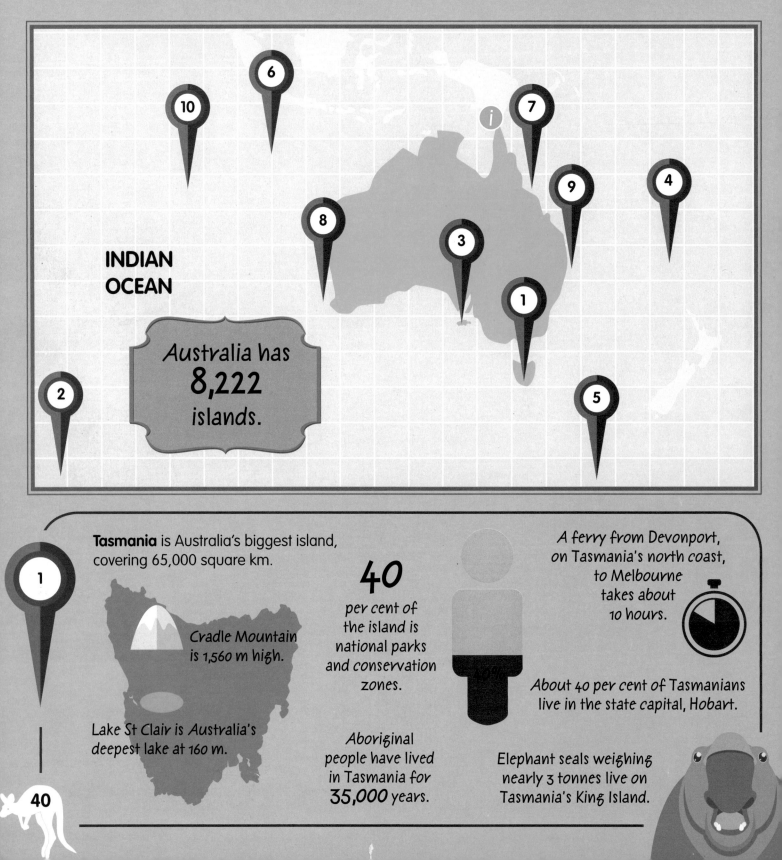

INDIAN OCEAN

Australia has **8,222** islands.

Tasmania is Australia's biggest island, covering 65,000 square km.

Cradle Mountain is 1,560 m high.

Lake St Clair is Australia's deepest lake at 160 m.

40 per cent of the island is national parks and conservation zones.

Aboriginal people have lived in Tasmania for **35,000** years.

A ferry from Devonport, on Tasmania's north coast, to Melbourne takes about 10 hours.

About 40 per cent of Tasmanians live in the state capital, Hobart.

Elephant seals weighing nearly 3 tonnes live on Tasmania's King Island.

2 The islands furthest from Australia are **Heard** and **McDonald Islands**, which are 4,100 km southwest of Perth.

The active volcano on Heard Island is called Big Ben.

3 **Kangaroo Island**, South Australia, is the country's third largest island.

Despite its name, Kangaroo Island's most famous animals are the sea lions around Seal Bay.

4 **Norfolk Island** is 1,610 km east of Sydney and has 1,800 residents.

Because so many surnames are shared, some residents are in the phone directory under their nicknames, such as Lettuce Leaf, Spuddy, Diddles and Loppy.

What's funny about that?

5 **Macquarie Island** is 1,500 km southeast of Tasmania. It's the only place in the world where rocks from the Earth's mantle, 6 km below the ocean floor, are exposed above sea level.

6 **Christmas Island**, in the Indian Ocean near to Java, was named by English sea captain William Mynors on **Christmas Day** in 1643.

7 **Magnetic Island** got its name because Captain Cook thought the island's granite rocks had magnetic powers.

8 **Rottnest Island** is so-called because Europeans thought the island was infested with big rats ('Rottnest' is 'rat's nest' in Dutch). The animal they saw was actually a type of wallaby called a **quokka**.

9 **Fraser Island**, off the coast of Queensland, is the world's largest sand island. It measures 1,600 square km.

10 The **Cocos Islands** are named after the vast coconut trees there.

i The **Torres Strait Islands**, between Australia and Papua New Guinea, are made up of over 70 small islands.

The Torres Strait has had its own flag since 1992.

On its flag, **green** represents the land, **blue** the sea and **black** the people. The **white** headdress is a symbol for the Torres Strait Islander people and the star is for the five major island groups.

Aussie traditions

Australians celebrate several special days throughout the year, such as ANZAC Day and Australia Day. There are also traditional festivals, events and sporting occasions celebrated by thousands of people.

The **Sydney New Year's Eve firework celebrations** are famous around the world.

Over 1 million spectators in Sydney Harbour

25,000 shooting comets

12,000 shells

Estimated $7 million cost

7 tonnes of fireworks

25 APRIL

ANZAC Day

It's a national public holiday and a time to remember Australians and New Zealanders who've lost their lives in conflicts around the world.

Dawn services are held at war memorials around Australia.

26 JANUARY

Australia Day

Marks the anniversary of British ships, known as the First Fleet, arriving in New South Wales in 1788. In 1934 all states and territories celebrated the day and it's been a public holiday since 1994.

26 MAY

National Sorry Day

First marked in 1998. It commemorates Indigenous Australian and Torres Strait Islander children who were wrongfully taken from their families by the government in the 19th and 20th centuries.

Some people think Australia Day should be celebrated on a different date, as January 26 marks the start of Indigenous Australian and Torres Strait Islander people being treated badly by Europeans.

1 SEPTEMBER

Wattle Day

This celebrates the wattle, Australia's national flower. Australian sports teams often wear green and gold because it signifies the golden wattle.

The tropical north Queensland towns of Tully, Innisfail and Babinda traditionally compete to see which town is the **wettest in Australia** each year.

- Tully holds the record with 7.9 metres of rain in 1950
- The competition is represented by a giant 7.9-metre-tall gumboot statue in Tully

The **Festival of the Winds** takes place every September on Bondi Beach. Multicultural music and dancing happens along the beach as well as market stalls, face painting and jumping castles.

Hundreds of large, colourful kites are flown in the sky.

It's become a tradition for international visitors to Australia to celebrate **Christmas** at Sydney's Bondi Beach.

Around **40,000** people visit the beach on 25 December, many dressed as **Santa Claus**.

The **Melbourne Marathon** takes place every October as part of the Melbourne Marathon Festival.

The marathon race is 26.2 miles long (42.195 km).

There is also a half marathon, 10 km run, 5.7 km run and 3 km fun run.

There is a $20,000 prize for the male and female marathon winner.

26 DECEMBER

First day of the **Boxing Day Test** between the Australian cricket team and another international team.

First day of the **Sydney to Hobart Yacht Race**, starting from Sydney Harbour.

Great government

Australia's Federal Parliament was formed in May 1901. It's controlled by central (federal) government and by individual states. Here you can discover all the Prime Ministers plus lots of fun facts about the government and its laws.

The **British monarch** remains the head of state in Australia.

Australia's Prime Ministers

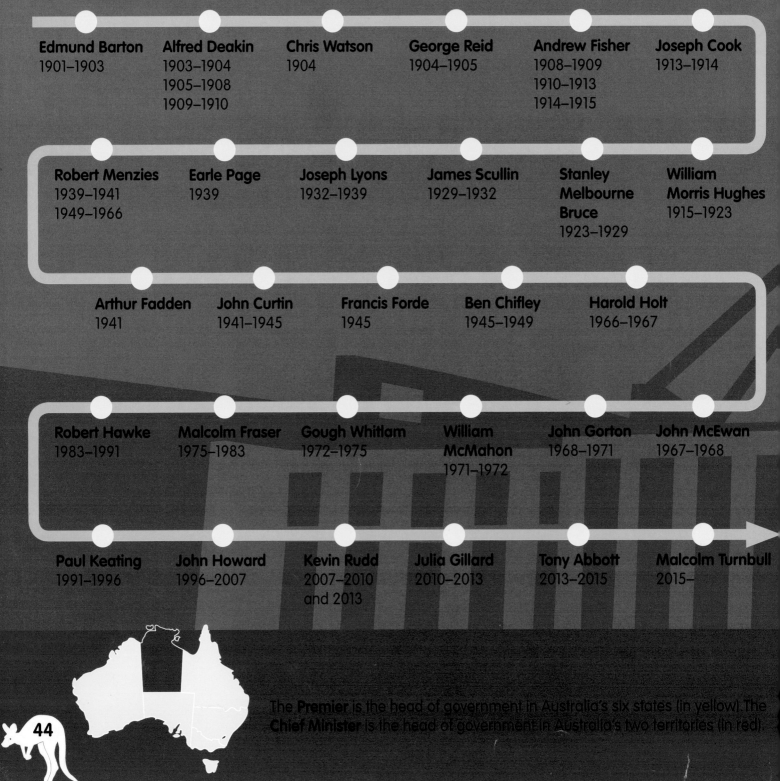

Edmund Barton
1901–1903

Alfred Deakin
1903–1904
1905–1908
1909–1910

Chris Watson
1904

George Reid
1904–1905

Andrew Fisher
1908–1909
1910–1913
1914–1915

Joseph Cook
1913–1914

Robert Menzies
1939–1941
1949–1966

Earle Page
1939

Joseph Lyons
1932–1939

James Scullin
1929–1932

Stanley Melbourne Bruce
1923–1929

William Morris Hughes
1915–1923

Arthur Fadden
1941

John Curtin
1941–1945

Francis Forde
1945

Ben Chifley
1945–1949

Harold Holt
1966–1967

Robert Hawke
1983–1991

Malcolm Fraser
1975–1983

Gough Whitlam
1972–1975

William McMahon
1971–1972

John Gorton
1968–1971

John McEwan
1967–1968

Paul Keating
1991–1996

John Howard
1996–2007

Kevin Rudd
2007–2010
and 2013

Julia Gillard
2010–2013

Tony Abbott
2013–2015

Malcolm Turnbull
2015–

The **Premier** is the head of government in Australia's six states (in yellow). The **Chief Minister** is the head of government in Australia's two territories (in red).

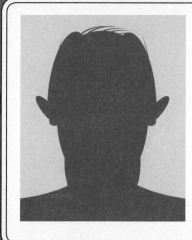

In 2017 the Prime Minister's salary was **$507,338** a year.

You can write to the Prime Minister by sending a letter to:

Prime Minister

Parliament House

Canberra ACT 2600

Or sending an email via the website: **www.pm.gov.au/contact-your-pm**

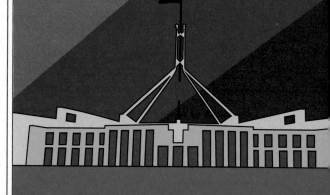

Francis Forde was Prime Minister for just **eight days**.

8
DAYS

In Australia it's illegal for any eligible citizen not to vote in federal elections, by-elections and referendums.

Robert Menzies was Prime Minister for 18 years, 5 months and 12 days.

18 YEARS | **5** MONTHS | **12** DAYS

Must be
18
or older to vote.

The Senate has **76** senators and the House of Representatives has **150** elected representatives. Together they make laws in the Australian Federal Parliament.

The **G20** is an annual meeting of the world's richest countries. The 2014 G20 was in Brisbane and PM Tony Abbott posed with world leaders cuddling **koalas**!

Strange laws

In South Australia it's against the law to **disrupt a wedding or a funeral**.

Until 1 July 2016, Western Australia's Potato Marketing Corporation could stop a vehicle they suspected of **carrying more than 50 kg of potatoes**.

Before 1902 it was illegal to **swim at beaches** during daylight.

45

Lay of the land

Covering more than 7 million square kilometres, Australia packs so much geographical greatness into its stunning landscapes. You'll discover stacks of fascinating facts here.

Australia is the world's **6th largest country** after Russia, Canada, China, the USA and Brazil.

Makes up **5 per cent** of the planet's land area.

Australia and its 8,222 islands cover **7,692,024** square km. That's about 32 times bigger than Great Britain.

×32

Western Australia	**2,529,875** sq km
Queensland	**1,730,648** sq km
Northern Territory	**1,349,129** sq km
South Australia	**983,482** sq km
New South Wales	**800,642** sq km
Victoria	**227,416** sq km
Tasmania	**68,401** sq km
Australian Capital Territory	**2,358** sq km

There are over **500 national parks** in Australia, covering 28 million hectares and 4 per cent of the land.

The country's national parks are found in mountains, deserts, forests and reefs.

Papua New Guinea
3.7 km

The country of **Papua New Guinea** is just **3.7 km** from Australia at their nearest points.

14 M high
110 M long

Australia is the lowest continent in the world with an average elevation of just **330 metres** above sea level.

Wave Rock in Western Australia was formed 2.7 billion years ago. It was made by weather and water erosion.

The lowest point is **Lake Eyre**, South Australia, which is **15 metres** below sea level.

New South Wales has a border **4,635 km** long and adjoins Queensland, South Australia, Victoria, Australian Capital Territory and Jervis Bay Territory.

No exact point marks the **centre of Australia** because the country is so vast, irregular shaped and curved by the Earth's surface.

Five suggested points for the centre are within 300 km of Alice Springs, Northern Territory.

Australia is drifting towards the equator by about **7 cm** every year.

Alice Springs

7 cm

Most northerly
Cape York, Queensland

Most westerly
Steep Point, Western Australia

N
W E
S

Most easterly
Cape Byron, New South Wales

The country is approximately
4,000 km from east to west and
3,200 km from north to south.

Jervis Bay **Territory** is a tiny coastal territory about 200 km east of Canberra.

Most southerly
South East Cape, Tasmania

Mount Twynam

Carruthers Peak

Alice Rawson Peak
Mount Townsend
Byatts Camp
Abbott Peak

New Zealand
2,000 km

Mount Kosciuszko, in New South Wales, is the highest point on mainland Australia.

2,228 m above sea level

The 10 highest mountains are all within 12 km of each other.

12 km

Mount Kosciuszko

Unnamed Peak

Rams Head North

Rams Head

It's often thought that Australia is close to **New Zealand**, but they're about 2,000 km apart.

That's the distance between London and Kiev in Ukraine.

ERUPTING VOLCANO

Australia is the only **continent** with **no active volcano**.

Mount Gambier, in South Australia, last erupted about **6,000** years ago.

SURFING

Australian Capital Territory is the only state or territory that doesn't have a coastline.

Oceans, seas and rivers

From the world famous Great Barrier Reef to huge lakes and basins, the oceans, seas and rivers of Australia are alive with amazing facts and stories. It's time to jump in …

Australia is surrounded by the
- Pacific Ocean
- Indian Ocean
- Arafura Sea
- Timor Sea
- Coral Sea
- Tasman Sea

In the hot summer month of January, the average water temperature is around

Gold Coast = 26°C

Perth = 22°C

Hobart = 16°C

More than **1,500 fish species** are found around the reef, including wobbegongs, manta rays, potato cod and beaked coralfish. Even great white sharks visit.

The **Great Barrier Reef**, off the coast of Queensland, stretches for **2,300 kilometres** over about **350,000 square kilometres**. It covers over 2,000 islands and nearly 3,000 separate reefs. It's the largest reef system in the world.

30 shipwrecks have been recorded around the reef.

$200 million

The amount the Australian and Queensland governments spend each year to protect the health of the Great Barrier Reef.

The **Great Barrier Reef Marine Park** carefully looks after the area and works hard to stop pollution affecting the reef. It teaches people to preserve the coral and has strict rules on what can be done in the water and on the islands.

Coral is formed by minute marine animals called **polyps**. Coral thrives in shallow water with good sunlight and low nutrients.

The reef began to form about 18,000 years ago during the last Ice Age.

A government group called the Reef Trust is working to control the population of crown-of-thorn starfish, which attack and eat the reef.

2 million
The number of visitors each year

The **Torres Strait** separates the far north of Australia from Papua New Guinea.

- *About 150 km wide*
- *Named after Portuguese explorer Luis Vaz de Torres who passed through it in 1606*

Timor Sea

Indian Ocean

Arafura Sea

Australia's longest rivers

River	Length	River	Length
Murray River	2,508 km	Lachlan River	1,339 km
Murrumbidgee River	1,485 km	Cooper Creek	1,113 km
Darling River	1,545 km	Flinders River	1,004 km
		Diamantia River	941 km

Great Barrier Reef

Flinders River

The **Lake Eyre basin** covers about 15 per cent of Australia and draws water from 1.2 million sq km. When it rains and the basin floods, between **6 to 8 million birds** flock to it.

There are 208 major waterways in Western Australia.

- *48 are wild rivers, which means they don't have barriers or dams*

Diamantia River

Coopey Creek

Coral Sea

The Commonwealth Scientific and Industrial Research Organisation (CSIRO) works to protect rare species around Lake Eyre, such as the night parrot, grey falcon and letter-winged kite.

Darling River

Lachlan River

Murrumbidgee River

Pacific Ocean

Murray River

Between November and March, **Blue Lake** at Mount Gambier in South Australia changes from dull grey to a bright blue. This could be because of the lake's water temperature.

The **largest man-made reservoir** in Australia is at Lake Gordon, in Tasmania. It holds **12,450 million cubic metres** of water and is used for water supplies and generating electricity.

It's more than 71 times bigger than the Corin reservoir in the Australian Capital Territory.

Berry's Canal, by the Shoalhaven River near Sydney, was Australia's first riverboat transport canal. It was 190 metres long and took just 12 days to build in 1822.

Tasman Sea

The Bass Strait is the stretch of water between Victoria and the island of Tasmania.

About 250 km wide.

Formed 12,000 years ago when the water level rose and separated Tasmania from mainland Australia.

WELCOME TO
MOUNT GAMBIER
WELCOME TO

Big business

If you're looking to spend money on goods and services such as cars, air travel, food, clothes and communications, these big Australian companies will help you splash the cash.

Qantas is Australia's national airline and began in 1920. Its name stands for **Q**ueensland **A**nd **N**orthern **T**erritory **A**erial **S**ervices.

- Has around 300 aircraft
- Carries nearly 50 million passengers a year
- Employs over 30,000 people
- Nicknamed 'The Flying Kangaroo'

The **BHP mining company** is one of Australia's biggest businesses. It was founded in 1885 in Broken Hill, New South Wales.

- Mines resources like coal, iron ore, copper and uranium
- Employs 65,000 people with $30 billion annual sales
- Nicknamed 'The Big Australian'

Australian surfer Brian Smith established the fashionable **UGG boots** brand in 1978.

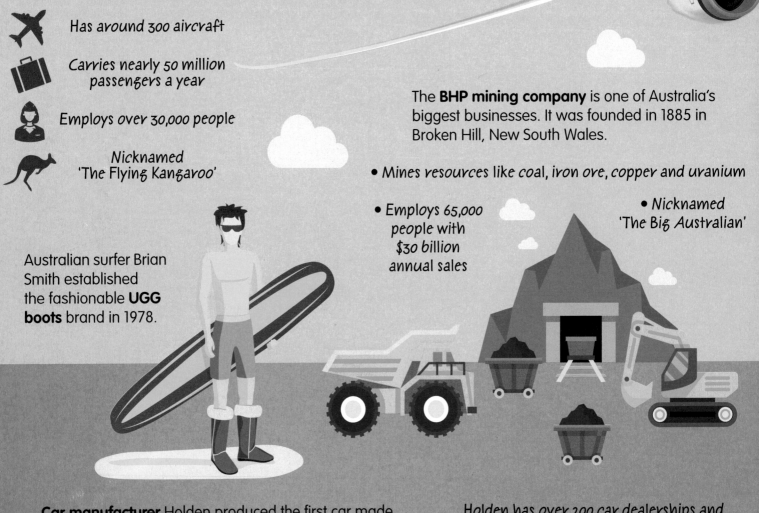

Car manufacturer Holden produced the first car made entirely in Australia in 1948.

Holden has over 200 car dealerships and 14,000 employees across Australia.

Holden originally began as a leatherwork and horse saddlery business in 1856 in Adelaide.

The top-of-the-range Holden Ute SS vehicle can reach

240 kph.

12 million

The approximate number of Australians in employment.

Healthcare and social assistance
1.5 million

Retail
1.22 million

Construction
1.08 million

Professional, scientific and technical
1.02 million

Education and training
957,000

Australia's biggest companies in 2016

	(yearly sales)
Wesfarmers (food, property, industrial)	**$66.2 billion**
Woolworths (retail)	**$58.5 billion**
Commonwealth Bank	**$44.3 billion**
Westpac Banking Corporation	**$37.6 billion**
NAB (banking)	**$36.6 billion**

There are more than 100 **Cold Rock ice cream** stores throughout Australia.

- The first ice cream shop opened in Aspley, Queensland, in 1996

- Over 30 million customers in 20 years

The famous **Speedo** swimwear manufacturer was founded in Sydney in 1914 and has a well-known boomerang logo.

Famous supermarkets **Woolworths** and **Coles** have over 60 per cent of the grocery market in the country.

787 Coles stores

995 Woolworths stores

Telstra is Australia's biggest telecommunications company. It provides mobile phone, app, internet, data and Pay TV services.

Tel (from 'telecoms') + **stra** (from 'Australia') = **Telstra**

51

Picturesque parks

Australia's national parks are large protected areas of unspoilt landscapes and amazing animals, plants and natural wonders. Thousands of visitors flock to these vast areas and admire the special scenery.

The most famous sight in the **Purnululu National Park**, in Western Australia, is the **Bungle Bungle Range**. It is a collection of beehive-shaped sandstone towers.

Formed over a period of 20 million years

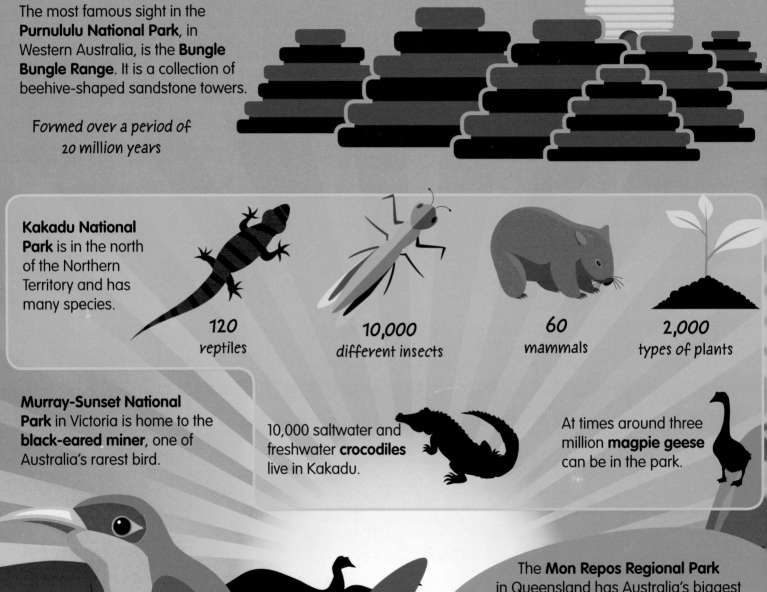

I'm sure the hive was somewhere round here.

Kakadu National Park is in the north of the Northern Territory and has many species.

120
reptiles

10,000
different insects

60
mammals

2,000
types of plants

Murray-Sunset National Park in Victoria is home to the **black-eared miner**, one of Australia's rarest bird.

10,000 saltwater and freshwater **crocodiles** live in Kakadu.

At times around three million **magpie geese** can be in the park.

The **Mon Repos Regional Park** in Queensland has Australia's biggest population of nesting **loggerhead turtles**.

Between November and March people can go on special trips to observe the turtles hatching and nesting their young.

The **Royal National Park**, near Sydney, was established in 1879.

The Figure Eight Pools are pretty rock pools by the coast, including one in a figure of eight shape.

Figure Eight Pools

The Twelve Apostles are a series of stunning limestone stacks on the coast of the **Port Campbell National Park** in Victoria.

The stacks were named after the Bible's twelve apostles.

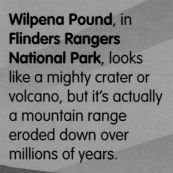
The Twelve Apostles

Wilpena Pound, in **Flinders Rangers National Park**, looks like a mighty crater or volcano, but it's actually a mountain range eroded down over millions of years.

Wilpena Pound

The **KULLA National Park** (Queensland) is named after the four Indigenous Australian groups who the land belongs to.

K Kaanju
U Umpila
L
L Lama Lama
A Ayapathu

The **Uluru-Kata Tjuta National Park**, in Northern Territory, is sacred to Aboriginal people.

It is home to the Uluru (Ayers Rock) sandstone rock formation.

Kata Tjuta are 36 huge rock domes, 32 km from Uluru.

Kata Tjuta is a Pitjantjatjara word which means 'many heads'.

Australia has 19 special **World Heritage** areas, including Kakadu, Uluru-Kata Tjuta and Purnululu National Parks.

Tourists and visitors

Millions of overseas visitors come to Australia each year to soak up its wonderful weather, exciting cities and amazing attractions. From the Great Barrier Reef to Sydney Harbour Bridge, there's so much to keep the tourists busy …

Australia's **tourism industry** is worth **$116.7** billion a year.

Sydney Airport is the busiest in the country. It received **41.87 million passengers** in 2016.

20 minutes
The average time it takes for a train or taxi to reach Sydney city centre from Sydney Airport.

300
Over **300 cruise ships** visit Sydney each year.

8.4 million international visitors come to Australia each year.

These visitors stay for **251 million** nights in total

Overseas visitors spend approximately **$39.8 billion**

Chinese visitors spend the most at **$9.7 billion.**

Where most visitors come from: (per year)

New Zealand	1.35 million
China	1.22 million
USA	726,800
UK	715,600
Singapore	437,800
Japan	423,800

States and territories that **international visitors** come to:

New South Wales	3.76 million
Victoria	2.63 million
Queensland	2.55 million
Western Australia	921,000
South Australia	430,000
Northern Territory	293,000
Tasmania	229,000
ACT	207,000

Each year visitors spend about **2.79 million days** exploring and learning about the fascinating plants and wildlife around the **Great Barrier Reef Marine Park**.

1606
The year of the first recorded visit of a European to Australia. **Dutch explorer** Willem Janszoon, and his ship the *Duyfken*, landed in Cape York.

54
The estimated number of **European ships** that visited Australia between 1606 and 1770.

Over 11 million visitors come to the **Gold Coast** each year.

11 million

Visitors can book a **'BridgeClimb'** to walk to the top of **Sydney Harbour Bridge**.

Climb
1,332
steps

Takes about
3.5
hours

Reach
134 m
at the top

Over **3 million people** have walked up Sydney Harbour Bridge.

Dreamworld, on the Gold Coast, is Australia's **biggest adventure theme park**. Over 8 million passengers have ridden its famous Tower of Terror II ride.

Reaches 161 kph in just 7 seconds, which is about the same as a Ferrari 458 sports car

100-m vertical free-fall drop

Royal visitors Prince William, the Duchess of Cambridge and baby Prince George visited Australia for 10 days in 2014.

There are **580,200 people employed** directly in tourism-related industries.

On the move

Australia's first steam trains began moving in the 1850s, and the country has been on the move ever since. It now boasts some of the world's most advanced public transport systems, mighty roads and millions of vehicles.

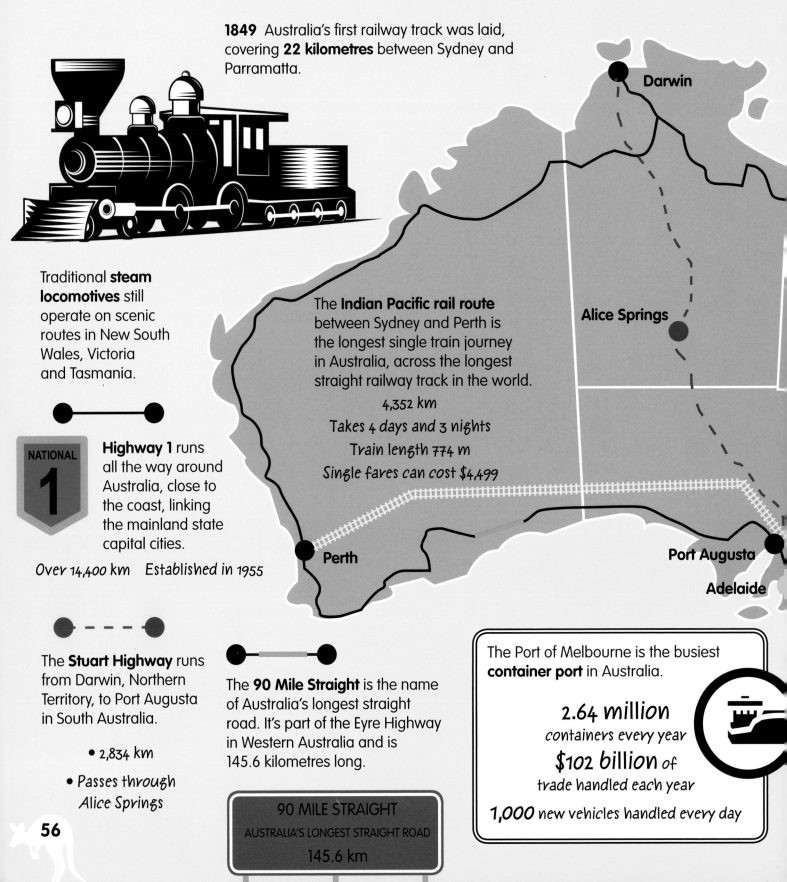

1849 Australia's first railway track was laid, covering **22 kilometres** between Sydney and Parramatta.

Traditional **steam locomotives** still operate on scenic routes in New South Wales, Victoria and Tasmania.

Highway 1 runs all the way around Australia, close to the coast, linking the mainland state capital cities.

Over 14,400 km   Established in 1955

The **Stuart Highway** runs from Darwin, Northern Territory, to Port Augusta in South Australia.

- 2,834 km
- Passes through Alice Springs

The **90 Mile Straight** is the name of Australia's longest straight road. It's part of the Eyre Highway in Western Australia and is 145.6 kilometres long.

90 MILE STRAIGHT
AUSTRALIA'S LONGEST STRAIGHT ROAD
145.6 km

The **Indian Pacific rail route** between Sydney and Perth is the longest single train journey in Australia, across the longest straight railway track in the world.

4,352 km

Takes 4 days and 3 nights

Train length 774 m

Single fares can cost $4,499

Darwin

Alice Springs

Perth

Port Augusta

Adelaide

The Port of Melbourne is the busiest **container port** in Australia.

2.64 million containers every year

$102 billion of trade handled each year

1,000 new vehicles handled every day

There are over **18 million** registered **vehicles** in Australia. The average age of a vehicle in Australia is 10 years.

76% petrol powered
22% diesel powered
2% other

110 kph

The maximum speed limit on most motorways, freeways and highways.

In 2016, Toyota sold the most new vehicles in Australia in total.

Toyota	209,610
Mazda	118,217
Hyundai	101,555
Holden	94,308
Ford	81,207

Some countries that drive on the **left** side of the road …

Australia	Japan	South Africa
India UK	New Zealand	Thailand

Cairns

The **RiverCat ferry** service between Circular Quay, Sydney and Parramatta takes 50 minutes.

The **Sydney Metro** public transport is due to open in **2019**.

First stage will cost
$8.3 billion
to construct

31 metro stations

Potential to transport
40,000 people an hour

Over **65 km** of new metro rail

Brisbane

Sydney

Melbourne trams

Melbourne **trams** have 250 kilometres of double track – the world's largest operating tram network

More than 1,700 tram stops

Average speed of tram is 16 kph

203 million tram journeys a year

$0 The cost of travelling on Melbourne's trams within the city's Free Tram Zone.

An electronic ticket called a myki can be touched on and off when using Melbourne's trains, trams and buses.

Melbourne

Hobart

Amazing plants and flowers

Exploring incredible countryside, rainforests and deserts reveals all sorts of interesting stories, facts and snippets of information. Many of these plants and flowers are unique to Australia.

24,000

The number of native plant species across all of Australia. In comparison, the UK has only 1,400.

Australia 24,000	
UK 1,400	

The World Wide Fund for Nature classes Australia as having **seven different ecosystems**. Deserts and shrub lands are the largest, across Western Australia, Northern Territory, South Australia and small western areas of Queensland and New South Wales.

The tropical and subtropical forests on the northeast Queensland coast covered most of Australia 15 million years ago.

The Royal Botanic Garden Sydney

8,900
plant species

67,100
plant specimens

3,964
trees

1.2 million
preserved plant species

Australia has over 30 types of **spinifex** grass across its huge deserts.

Rainforests on the east coast cover 0.3 per cent of Australia's land.

- Over 18,000 plant species
  - Some trees are over 2,500 years old

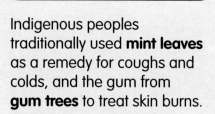

Indigenous peoples traditionally used **mint leaves** as a remedy for coughs and colds, and the gum from **gum trees** to treat skin burns.

The hot and dry desert centre of Australia supports around 2,000 plant species.

Spinifex stores water and needs frequent exposure to fires to survive.

Golden wattle is the national flower of Australia. It's called wattle because early European settlers used its thin branches to create 'wattle and daub' mud buildings.

- 954 different species of wattle grow in Australia
- In 1912, wattle became part of the Australian coat of arms

The kangaroo paw flower is Western Australia's floral symbol.

Spring
(August to November) in Western Australia

- Over **11,000** species of wild flowers bloom
- **75 per cent** only grow in this state

DEC | JAN | FEB
NOV
OCT
SEP
AUG | JUL | JUN
MAY
APR
MAR

The **boab tree**, which grows in dry parts of Western and Northern Australia, is easy to spot because of its large swollen trunk.

- Can store over 100,000 litres of water in its trunk
- Sheds leaves in the dry season to survive

Australia's **eucalyptus trees** are the tallest trees in the country. The tallest of all is called Centurion and is in Tasmania's Arve Valley.

- 99.6 metres tall
- 30 metres taller than the Sydney Opera House

Eucalyptus trees are nicknamed 'gum trees' and about **700** varieties are only found in Australia.

The **Wollemi pine tree** was only discovered in New South Wales in 1994.

It was thought to have become extinct between **65 and 200 million** years ago.

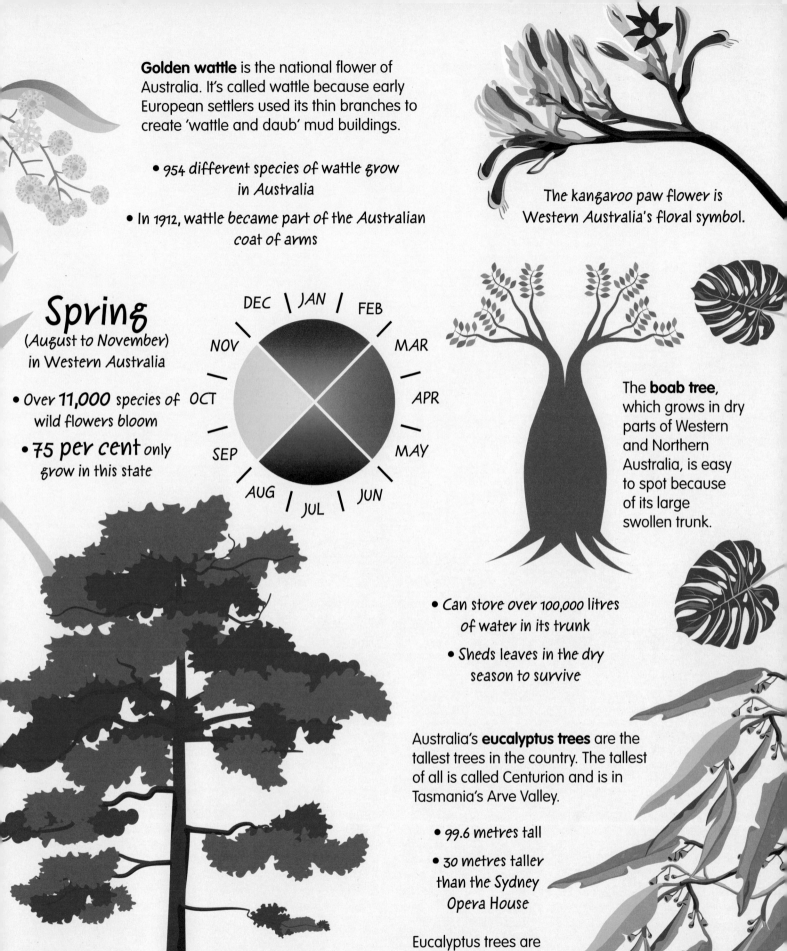

Going underground

Australia's 'gold rush' began in the 1850s, when European settlers mined for gold in search of their fortune. The country has plentiful natural resources and materials are extracted from the ground and taken all over the world.

Gold was discovered near Bathurst, New South Wales, in 1851. More finds were made soon after at Bendigo and Ballarat in Victoria. Gold was found in Western Australia in the 1890s.

The Boddington Gold Mine, in Western Australia, is the largest in the country. It's produced more than **56.6 tonnes of gold**.

Nugget = a large piece of gold

Gold dust = a tiny piece

114 gold mines

Produces **272** tonnes a year

World's second largest producer, behind China

$14 billion of gold exports

Silver was discovered around the outback city of Broken Hill, New South Wales, in the 1880s. Broken Hill is still Australia's largest producer of silver, zinc and lead minerals.

25 per cent of the silver that's mined is refined and sent to Japan.

In 1966, Australia's 50-cent coin was the last in the world in general use to contain silver.

The Argyle Diamond Mine, in the Kimberley region in Western Australia, produces over 90 per cent of the world's pink and red **diamonds**.

The mine could close in 2020 when all the rocks containing diamonds have been extracted.

Lithium is a soft, silver-white metal that's become very important in the use of batteries for mobile phones and tablets.

Australia has about 11 per cent of the world's lithium resources.

Australia provides 30 per cent of the world's **coal**. Coal is a fossil fuel burnt to make energy.

Australia has enough coal reserves to continue production for 100 years.

It exports nearly 300 million tonnes of coal per year.

It earns around $35 billion a year by exporting coal.

Huge **bucket-wheel excavator machines**, used to dig open-pit coal mines, can be 45 metres high with a saw 12 metres in diameter.

Iron ore is found in rocks 600 million years old.

Australia is the world's largest iron ore producer.

95 per cent of iron ore comes from the Pilbara region in Western Australia.

Iron ore is mainly used to make steel.

In 2001, an enormous industrial train taking iron ore from Western Australia's mines reached the **Port Hedland** harbour.

Western Australia	99,734 tonnes of iron ore	Port Hedland
	682 wagons	
	7.35 km long	

Er, I think we've made the train a bit too long.

The town of Coober Pedy, South Australia, is called the 'Opal Capital of the World'. Precious **opal** was discovered in 1915 and 70 per cent of the world's opal comes from here.

With temperatures often over 40°C, many Coober Pedy houses are underground or built in rocks, where it's much cooler.

The world's largest opal, weighing 5.27 kg, was discovered in Coober Pedy.

Australia's two main **copper** deposits are at the Olympic Dam in South Australia and Mount Isa in Queensland.

Australia has about **6 per cent** of the world's copper resources. Chile has the most at 25 per cent.

Copper is found in rocks more than **250 million** years old.

Most copper is used in electrical systems, motors and wires.

More minerals found in Australia

 graphite

bauxite

nickel

manganese

shale oil

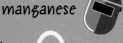 phosphate

tin

thorium

tungsten

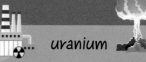 uranium

Australia: more things to find

This is Australia is jammed with hundreds of fascinating facts, stats, events and stories all about this amazing place. Here, you'll find even more useful website addresses and links so that you can explore one of the world's most incredible countries even further.

Before you go …
It's a good idea to check the website of, or telephone, the place or attraction you're visiting, just to make sure it isn't closed or has any restrictions. You don't want to make a long journey, only to have a nasty surprise when you arrive!

Sports
Melbourne Cricket Ground: www.mcg.org.au
Australian Football League: www.afl.com.au
Australian Soccer team: www.socceroos.com.au
Sydney Olympic Stadium (Stadium Australia): www.anzstadium.com.au
Melbourne Park (Australian Open tennis venue): www.ausopen.com
WACA Ground (Western Australian Cricket Association): www.waca.com.au
Commonwealth Games 2018, Gold Coast: www.gc2018.com

Arts and culture
National Gallery of Australia, Canberra: www.nga.gov.au
Sydney Opera House: www.sydneyoperahouse.com
Australian Museum, Sydney: www.australianmuseum.net.au
Perth International Arts Festival: www.perthfestival.com.au
National Museum Australia, Canberra: www.nma.gov.au
Australian Government: www.australia.gov.au/information-and-services/culture-and-arts
New South Wales tourism: www.sydney.com/things-to-do/arts-and-culture
Australian Library and Information Association: www.alia.org.au
William Ricketts Sanctuary, Victoria: www.parkweb.vic.gov.au/explore/parks/william-ricketts-sanctuary-gardens-of-the-dandenongs

Parks and gardens
Great Barrier Reef Marine Park: www.gbrmpa.gov.au
National Parks (Government): www.australia.gov.au/about-australia/australian-story/national-parks
Parks Australia: www.parksaustralia.gov.au
New South Wales National Parks: www.nationalparks.nsw.gov.au/visit-a-park
Australian National Parks (tourism): www.australia.com/en-gb/articles/australias-national-parks.html
Uluru-Kata Tjuta National Park: www.parksaustralia.gov.au/uluru
KULLU National Park: www.npsr.qld.gov.au/parks/kulla-mcilwraith-range
Royal Botanical Gardens, Sydney: www.rbgsyd.nsw.gov.au

Historic attractions
Endeavour ship replica, Sydney: www.anmm.gov.au/whats-on/vessels/hmb-endeavour
Royal Flying Doctors Broken Hill Base and museum, New South Wales: www.flyingdoctor.org.au/nswact/our-services
Aboriginal rock art in the Kimberley, Western Australia: www.kimberleyfoundation.org.au
Old Melbourne Gaol: www.oldmelbournegaol.com.au

Helpful groups

Australian Government: www.australia.gov.au
Tourism Australia: www.australia.com
New South Wales Tourism: www.sydney.com
Queensland Tourism: www.queensland.com
Melbourne and Victoria Tourism: www.visitvictoria.com
Western Australia Tourism: www.tourism.wa.gov.au
South Australia Tourism: www.tourism.sa.gov.au
Northern Territory Tourism: www.tourismnt.com.au and www.northernterritory.com
Australian Capital Territory Tourism: www.tourism.act.gov.au
Tasmania Tourism: www.discovertasmania.com

Monuments and attractions

Uluṟu and Kata Tjuṯa: www.parksaustralia.gov.au/uluru/index.html
Dinosaur Stampede National Monument, Queensland: www.dinosaurtrackways.com.au
Australian Government (heritage and places): www.environment.gov.au/heritage/heritage-places
The Wheel of Brisbane: www.thewheelofbrisbane.com.au
Australian War Memorial, ACT: www.awm.gov.au
Sydney Harbour Bridge: www.australia.gov.au/about-australia/australian-story/sydney-harbour-bridge
Monuments Australia: www.monumentaustralia.org.au

Famous buildings

Parliament House, Canberra: www.aph.gov.au
Sydney Opera House: www.sydneyoperahouse.com
Royal Exhibition Building, Victoria: www.museumvictoria.com.au/reb
Q1 Tower, Brisbane: www.q1.com.au
Sydney Tower: www.sydneytowereye.com.au
The Bell Tower, Perth: www.thebelltower.com.au
Alice Springs Telegraph Station, Northern Territory: www.alicespringstelegraphstation.com.au

Full of fun

Dreamworld adventure park, Gold Coast: www.dreamworld.com.au
Climbing Sydney Harbour Bridge: www.bridgeclimb.com
Australia Zoo, Queensland: www.australiazoo.com.au
National Zoo and Aquarium, Canberra: www.nationalzoo.com.au
Streets Beach, Brisbane: www.visitbrisbane.com.au/brisbane/things-to-do/sport-and-recreation/beaches-and-lakes/
streets-beach
Puffing Billy steam train, Melbourne: www.puffingbilly.com.au
Sea World Gold Coast: www.seaworld.com.au

Out and about

Lake Burley Griffin, Canberra: www.visitcanberra.com.au/attractions
Bondi Beach, Sydney: www.australia.com/en-gb/places/nsw/nsw-bondi-beach.html
Snowy Mountains, New South Wales: www.snowymountains.com.au
Canberra Deep Space Communication Complex, ACT: www.cdscc.nasa.gov
Daintree Rainforest visitor centre, Queensland: www.discoverthedaintree.com
Skyrail Rainforest Cableway, Cairns: www.skyrail.com.au
Golden Mile Heritage Walk, Melbourne: www.visitmelbourne.com/regions/melbourne/things-to-do/tours

Index